THE
EXIT
FACTOR

THE EXIT FACTOR

BUILD PROFIT, GROW VALUE, AND EXIT ON YOUR TERMS

JESSICA FIALKOVICH

Copyright © 2025 by Jessica Fialkovich

All rights reserved.

No part of this publication may be reproduced or transmitted in any form or by any means, electronic or mechanical, including photography, recording, or any information storage and retrieval system, without permission in writing from the author.

Requests for permission to make copies of any part of the work should be emailed to the following address: jessica@exitfactor.com

Neither the publisher nor the author shall be liable for any loss of profit or any other commercial damages, including but not limited to special, incidental, consequential, personal, or other damages.

Published and distributed by EXF Press
Bedford, USA
exitfactor.com

Library of Congress Control Number: 2025912702
Fialkovich, Jessica
The Exit Factor: Build Profit, Grow Value, and Exit on Your Terms

ISBN:
Paperback 979-8-9992473-0-8
eBook 979-8-9992473-1-5

To the business owners who wake up early, stay up late, and carry more than most people will ever understand. This book is for you: the builders, the dreamers, the grinders. You created something from nothing, and now you're ready for what's next.

May this guide help you claim not just the value you've earned but the freedom you deserve.

And to my husband, Al, thank you for being my partner in every sense of the word. None of this would have been possible without your support, belief, and humor when I needed it most.

A NOTE ABOUT CONFIDENTIALITY

Nothing is more important to me than protecting the identity and details of clients I've served and entrepreneurs who have shared their stories with me. To that end, all the stories shared in this book have had details altered, including names, industries, and, in some cases, other key information, to protect their confidentiality.

CONTENTS

You're Going to Want This Before You Start		1
Introduction: The Illusion of Success		3
Why Growth Isn't Enough And What It Takes to Really Succeed		
1	Value-Growth Thinking	15
	How Successful Owners Think Differently	
2	The Three Stages of the Entrepreneur	33
	Founder – Builder – Investor	
3	The VORTEx Model	53
	Your Roadmap to Exit Readiness	
4	Phase 1: Value	77
	Define What You Want and What It's Worth	
5	Phase 2: Optimize Your Financials	111
	Increase Profit to Drive Value	
6	Phase 3: Record What You Do	139
	Build a Business That Runs Without You	
7	Phase 4: Transform Your Growth	167
	Scale Smarter and Faster	
8	Phase 5: Exit, But Not the End	205
	Scale Smarter and Faster	
9	The Next 90 Days	247
	Turn Your Exit Plan into Motion	
10	Own Your Business. Own Your Life.	263
Bonus 1: What to Do Next		267
Bonus 2: Your Business Challenges, Solved		271
Author's Note		275
Glossary of Terms		277
Acknowledgments		283

YOU'RE GOING TO WANT THIS BEFORE YOU START

This book isn't just something you read; it's something you *use*.

To help you put everything into action, I've created the **Exit Factor Toolkit,** a set of simple, powerful tools designed to guide you step by step through the strategies in this book.
Inside the toolkit, you'll get:

The Value Vision Map™ (VVM)

Define what you want from your business and what it will take to get there.

The Profit Pulse Plan™ (PPP)

Identify where your business is leaking money and how to plug the holes for good.

The Role Release Roadmap™ (3R)
Get clear on what you need to let go of and how to delegate without chaos, finally.

3-Growth Matrix™ (3GM)
Figure out how to easily grow your business without additional capital investment.

The Exit Prep Scorecard™ (XPS)
Choose the best path to exit your business and start building toward it now.

The Exit Assessment™ Overview
An overview of our comprehensive business valuation and planning report.

These are the exact tools I use with clients who pay tens of thousands for one-on-one guidance, and they're yours, free, as a reader of this book.

Download your toolkit at exitfactorbook.com
You'll also get access to our free community of business owners working through this program, so you never have to do it alone.

Introduction

THE ILLUSION OF SUCCESS

Why Growth Isn't Enough And What It Takes to Really Succeed

Chris didn't plan to build a fast-growing logistics firm. It began as a side project. A few consulting gigs evolved into several more. Before long, Chris was hiring staff, signing contracts, and building something bigger than he'd imagined.

From the outside, Chris was living the dream: a multimillion-dollar business, an excellent reputation in his industry, clients that most people would swoon over, and an experienced team that would make anyone jealous. He looked the part, dressed the part, heck, he even keynoted conferences on how to build a successful business.

But despite the appearance of success, the company was barely breaking even. Chris assumed that profits would naturally follow as revenue grew. Instead, the company's margins continued to shrink. Year after year, he was reinvesting in the business. And worse, he had recently patched financial gaps with lines of credit and personal savings.

By all accounts, he had achieved what many business owners dream of: a growing company, high-profile clients, and a whole team of experts running the day-to-day operations.

But behind the scenes, small cracks were blistering into bigger problems.

However, Chris had a plan. Everything would shift if he could land a few more large contracts and reach the next revenue goal. He even had a financial model to prove the theory. Once the company hit that next level, everything would shift, and the profits would flow.

Then he landed that next contract, and it didn't happen. Instead of moving forward, he sank further into the red. That's when I met Chris. He hired me to help position the company for long-term growth and attract investors to help steer it in the right direction. But it didn't take long to see the deeper issue.

From our first conversation, it was clear that Chris was conflicted about his plan.

On one hand, he was a true visionary: full of ideas, plans, and positivity for the future. In his mind, reaching profitability was inevitable. If he could just land that one ideal client, everything would be okay!

I love Chris and entrepreneurs like him. Entrepreneurship is like a rickety old wooden roller coaster at a run-down amusement park. You know it looks pretty dangerous, and you probably shouldn't ride it, but damn, it looks fun. So, you get on anyway. To put ourselves on that rickety roller coaster, we must be a bit insane and have an untenable amount of optimism, like Chris.

But other times, Chris was on the other side of the entrepreneurial coin. I could see it in his face as soon as he joined calls; hair a bit of a mess, eyes red with dark circles under them, and a look of defeat. I immediately recognized the look on Chris's face because I've seen it in the mirror more times than I can count. He was burnt out. Chris had taken the ride down that rollercoaster one too many times, and he couldn't take it anymore.

He wanted to go on a smoother ride. Spinning around on teacups seemed a better option than his current state of affairs. And this is the curse of entrepreneurship. At one time, we were filled with optimism, enthusiasm, and a zest for the business. But we can only take it for so long when we run a company that constantly drains our time, money, and freedom.

The Realization: This Isn't Sustainable

Chris wasn't running a business anymore. The company was running him.

Taking on an investor and growing the team and company meant he would have to double down on his efforts. And if he was being honest, how much harder could he possibly work?

So he started to ask a different question: "What would it take to step away from this?"

That's when we did an Exit Assessment (you'll learn more about this tool in a later chapter). It told Chris what his business was worth today and all the areas holding him back from reaching his goal.

The results were stunning. The company was a mess. For all the work he'd put in, the business wasn't worth nearly as much as he expected.

Discovering that the business was worth only a fraction of what he needed to step away was a total gut punch. Chris followed many entrepreneurs' blueprints: grow the top line, keep pushing, and assume that the value will take care of itself.

But he wasn't building a valuable business; he was building a treadmill.

Despite generating substantial revenue, the business had never achieved a significant profit. Chris was overpaying employees, undercharging clients, and doing too much work himself. It was exhausting, unsustainable, and, according to his valuation, worthless.

The truth is that Chris is not alone.

Most business owners fall into the same trap. The chase for "more," more clients, more employees, more sales, without a clear path for profit and value.

Our society as a whole focuses on more. It even spills into our personal lives: more clothes, cars, and square feet in our homes. But more doesn't deliver value, especially when it comes to business.

It wasn't his fault. Chris was using the playbook he had seen business owners follow before them: grow at all costs. And he had achieved what he set out to do, not realizing he was destroying his future.

That's why I wrote this book.

Before we dive in, I want to acknowledge something important:

You're busy. Probably overwhelmed. You didn't pick up this book because you've got hours of free time to kill; you picked it up because you're tired of your business running your life.

So yes, this book is a commitment. But it's a *different kind* of time commitment. Every chapter is designed to get you out of the weeds, off the treadmill, and closer to owning a business that works *for* you, not just because of you.

You won't find fluff here. I've distilled everything I've learned from helping thousands of business owners scale, optimize, and exit. And while you can skim parts of it, I promise: if you read it in order and apply what's inside, it will change the way you operate your business and your life.

So permit yourself to slow down just long enough to get clear.

The financial pain of an unvaluable business is obvious, but the emotional toll? It's just as brutal.

But it doesn't have to be that way.

Introducing the VORTEx

Working together, Chris and I laid out a roadmap for turning things around based on the concepts that we will cover together.

This book introduces the Exit Factor™ program and our five-phase VORTEx Model™, designed to give you time, money, and freedom as you grow your business and plan your exit.

V: Value

This phase helps you identify your long-term goals for the future of you and your company and how they compare to your current situation.

O: Optimize

Here we optimize the financial performance of your company, boosting your profits and giving you more dollars back in your pocket.

R: Record

Owning a business is not a job; however, you may hold one or more jobs in your business. In Record, we free up your time by systematically delegating roles and responsibilities off your plate.

T: Transform

Now that we have a profitable business model in place and the necessary personnel to execute the work, it's time to grow. However, not growth for growth's sake. In Transform, we focus on the activities that will produce the most significant long-term value.

Ex: Exit

Once you've completed all of the phases, you are ready to exit. In this last phase, we identify the ideal exit option, buyer, and team you will need to execute your goal.

When implemented in order, the five phases of the VORTEx Model help you clarify your goals, fix your financial model, document what's working, build a business that runs without you, and exit on your terms.

This method has been successful for companies of all sizes, ranging from those with annual revenues of $200,000 to those exceeding $25 million in revenue. It works across various industries, including professional services, manufacturing, and tech startups. Whether your business is just breaking the $500K mark or pushing past eight figures, the VORTEx applies. Why does it cross so many sections? Because the focus is to create business fundamentals and a model that supports its investors and owners (you)!

The secret? We reshape your business to operate like an investor-owned company, not an entrepreneur-run one.

When that shift happens, your company starts working *for you* instead of sucking the life out of you. It becomes the engine that delivers time, money, and freedom rather than draining it.

Entrepreneur vs. Investor: A New Lens

ENTREPRENEUR MODEL	INVESTOR MODEL
• Owner wears ten hats	• Defined leadership roles
• Systems are not documented or followed	• Documented, repeatable processes
• Growth focused on revenue	• Profitable, intentional growth
• Reactive, fire-drill mode	• Scalable, strategic operation

This book is broken down into three sections.

The first section is about **Preparing You** as an individual for this program. The entrepreneur who got you to where you are today will not be the same entrepreneur who gets you to the finish line. If you picked up this book, you have big goals.

I have overseen more than 1,500 exits in my career: some great, some truly awful and heartbreaking. The truth is that it was never the *business* that determined how the exit went; it was the *owner*. Before we embark on changing anything about your business, we must ensure **you** can make the journey.

These first two chapters are not the soft, fluffy stuff you will want to skip over. Mindset and identity are the keys to success in my industry.

Second, I will talk about **Preparing Your Business**. In this section, I provide detailed descriptions of each phase of the VORTEx Model. I will walk you through the purpose of each phase and some of the top tactics that we take our clients through to boost their profits and value. During this section, you will rely heavily on the toolset accompanying this book, which can be downloaded from exitfactorbook.com.

Last, I leave you with an **Implementation Guide**. This 90-day action plan provides you with direct actions you can implement in your business, tailored to your exit timeline.

Along the way, we'll revisit Chris's journey and show how he transformed his company. Spoiler: he didn't opt for the big exit he originally dreamed of. He achieved much more: freedom, profit, and peace of mind. And honestly? That's a better win than the one he thought he wanted.

Whether you want to exit, scale, or simply stop feeling like the bottleneck in your business, the VORTEx is how we get you there.

Stuck in the VORTEx? You're Not Alone.
"Where are *you* stuck in the VORTEx?"

- I'm working too much for too little
- I'm not sure what my business is worth
- I want out—but don't know how

(You'll find answers to all these in the chapters ahead.)

The Tornado: A Natural Force—and a Business Blueprint

There's a reason the Exit Factor logo and the VORTEx Model have a tornado theme (and it's not just my love for *Twister*). A tornado starts with chaos, narrows with clarity, and builds into something powerful enough to reshape everything in its path. It doesn't start on the ground. It begins high above, where warm, humid air collides with cooler, drier air in the upper atmosphere. This tension creates instability.

Then comes the updraft.

A funnel cloud emerges as rising air from a thunderstorm pulls that rotation down vertically. It's wide, loose, but gathering momentum. As the spin intensifies and the funnel narrows, energy becomes increasingly concentrated. Focus builds. And when that funnel finally touches the ground, the tornado makes an impact.

Yes, a tornado can destroy many homes, dreams, living creatures, and people (I do not take this lightly as I live and see this destruction every year as a resident of North Texas. I actually have a healthy fear and deep respect for Mother Nature and the damage she can cause). But nature always plays a dual role. Tornadoes also clear the dead wood. They churn the soil. In the aftermath, there's space, sometimes painful, for regeneration.

The impact and regeneration process of a tornado is what building a business looks like.

The energy begins at the top of the funnel: the dream. The idea. The "what if." It's all potential at this stage, broad, inspiring, but unfocused. As the business grows, that energy starts to narrow. Strategy is introduced. Systems are built. The right people are hired.

Every wise decision pulls that swirling energy down the funnel. What once was an abstract vision gains direction and speed.

And the base of that funnel? That's the exit.

The moment when all that energy, all that intention, and all that focus finally hit the ground. And if you've done it right, that exit—a sale, a succession, or a strategic transition—leaves a lasting impact. It clears the way for new growth for you, your team, your family, and the new leader.

Why This Book Matters

I believe in entrepreneurship. I believe it's the heartbeat of our economy. And I believe every owner deserves a win at the end of the journey, a moment when all the sacrifices finally pay off.

And that win? It's not just about you.

When a business shuts down, it has a profound impact on its employees, families, vendors, and the surrounding community. Clients often take their business elsewhere, usually to large, impersonal national firms. The local ripple effect is real.

This book is your guide. It wasn't developed in a vacuum, based on Harvard studies or theories from experts who have built and sold a single business, or maybe even none at all. What I'm sharing with you is a system I've created after living the entrepreneurial rollercoaster for almost two decades. Starting, growing, and selling (some) more than twenty-five different businesses. Some were wildly successful, while others were not. And along the way, helping thousands of other business owners do the same. I've taken lessons from my clients and businesses and incorporated them into effective tactics and strategies, packaged into a simple system to serve you, the entrepreneur.

The stakes are high. **Your exit isn't just about you. And you have an obligation to do it well. So let's get started.**

SECTION ONE

PREPARING YOU

Chapter 1

VALUE-GROWTH THINKING

How Successful Owners Think Differently

Trapped in the Business You Built

Have you ever stopped to ask yourself why it feels like the weight of your entire business is on your shoulders every day? You have clients, a team, and steady revenue. On paper, you're successful. But it doesn't *feel* like success.

You started this business with hope and excitement. It was supposed to be the key to a better life: to provide for your family, have the freedom to spend time with them, and build something meaningful for the future.

Instead, mornings start before the sun rises, answering emails while gulping down coffee, trying to get ahead before the demands of your household kick in. Once the kids are off to school, the absolute chaos begins: client meetings, team check-ins, project deadlines, fires to put out, deliverables to review, and countless emails that dominate your day, leaving no time to think, let alone breathe.

Even with a team, everything still seems to land on your desk. You're the decision-maker, the problem-solver, the one everyone turns to. And while you may have support in theory, you're still doing it all in reality.

You've built something incredible, but instead of freedom, you've become the linchpin holding it all together. On the outside, it looks like you have it all together. But inside? Inside, you feel like you're one bad day away from everything crumbling. It's a treadmill you can't seem to get off, and the harder you push, the faster it seems to go.

There is a way out. However, it requires stepping back and preparing for the moment when your business can thrive without you at its center.

The truth is, what you're doing now will never create the life you want. If you keep running your business the same way: if you keep holding on to every decision, every detail, every ounce of responsibility, you'll keep getting the same result: exhaustion, overwhelm, and no clear plan for the future.

It's not just about finding freedom for yourself. It's about transforming your business into the valuable asset it was always meant to be: an asset that generates wealth, fosters freedom, and leaves a lasting legacy.

The question is, are you ready to take that step?

I've seen thousands of business owners land in this exact place. According to entrepreneur Tony Robbins, **87% of business owners in the U.S. never achieve a successful exit**. They spend their lives working harder than their employees, sacrificing time with their families, and still walk away with little to show for it. They either burn out, shut down, or pass on a business that crumbles without them.

That's not the legacy you're building this for.

Entrepreneurial poverty isn't just a financial gap; it's also an emotional one. It's the anxiety of not taking a paycheck, the guilt of missing family moments, the burnout that builds when everyone else sees you as successful, but you feel like you're barely keeping it together. This chapter is your turning point. We're going to shift from survival to strategy.

The First Step to Freedom

So, how do you avoid becoming part of that 87%? How do you break free from the survival cycle and step into the small but mighty group of business owners who build something that genuinely works, becoming part of the Elite 13%™ who achieve a successful exit?

You start by thinking differently.

You start by seeing your business not as an extension of yourself but as a financial asset.

You start by adopting a new lens, one I call **Value-Growth Thinking.**

The Harsh Truth About Business Exits

The reality is harsh:

- More than **50%** of businesses fail in their first year.
- An estimated **70%** don't make it past their fifth year.
- Of the ones that do survive, as I mentioned, **87% never achieve a successful exit.**

Most business owners have no exit strategy at all. They assume they'll sell the business when they're ready to retire or pass it on to the next generation. But those assumptions rarely hold up.

Here's why:

- Selling to employees? Only **9%** want ownership.
- Hiring a CEO? The average CEO salary is **$183,270**, which is out of reach for most small- to mid-sized companies.
- Passing it down to family? Only **13%** of family businesses survive into the second generation.

What's left?

For most owners, it's shutting the doors and walking away from everything they built.

Unless…you take control now.

Why "More" Isn't the Answer

Like many entrepreneurs, you've likely bought into the myth that more is better; you grow every year, hire more people. It all sounds like progress, right? But more of the wrong things? They are a trap.

A few years ago, I decided to visit Disney World. It was supposed to be the perfect trip, a magical, memory-making experience everyone raves about. I had it all planned out: three days, four parks, every moment packed with character breakfasts, rides, and the most efficient walking routes through the parks. I had a spreadsheet and was determined to ensure we didn't miss *anything*.

The first day, we hit the ground running, literally. We were up at dawn, standing in line before the park opened, hustling from one ride to the next. By lunchtime, we'd already checked off half the rides on my list, but no one was having fun. My husband looked stressed, and I was so busy managing the schedule that I didn't even realize how exhausted I was. But I told myself, *it's fine. We'll just push through. It'll be worth it.*

By day three, we were done. My husband was over it. And I, well, I felt defeated. I had planned *everything* perfectly. We were doing *more* than most families could fit into a week. But instead of making memories, we were just making ourselves miserable.

When I returned home, all I could think about was that I had been so focused on doing everything that I missed out on what mattered most: being in the moment and connecting with the people I love.

So, when we planned a return trip this past year, I decided to do things differently.

This time, we'd focus on one fantastic day instead of trying to do *everything*. I booked a VIP tour, not something I would typically consider, but I wanted this trip to be about quality over quantity. It felt like a splurge, but I repeated my new mantra: value doesn't always equal price.

We didn't rush out the door at sunrise on the tour day. We had a relaxed breakfast together, laughing and discussing what we were most excited about. When we arrived at the park, our guide greeted us and whisked us past the crowds straight to the rides we'd chosen together, as a family.

We hit all the must-dos, the rides we had been dreaming about, without the stress of navigating lines or racing against the clock.

But what stood out wasn't the efficiency. It was the freedom. Instead of worrying about logistics, I got to experience the joy on everyone's faces. We had time to linger at favorite spots, take silly photos, and even ride Slinky Dog three times in a row.

We weren't exhausted; we were more connected as a family than ever. It was one of those rare days when everything felt magical. (I think this is what Disney is supposed to feel like?)

That experience taught me a lesson about business. It's not about how *much* you do, it's about doing the *right* things. In business, just like in life, you can create extraordinary outcomes when you focus your energy and resources on what truly matters, instead of trying to do it all. Sometimes, less but better is precisely what you need.

The right things, done intentionally, are what truly create value.

Chasing more feels good in the moment, but it doesn't build lasting value. It doesn't make your business more valuable to you or a future owner. And it doesn't bring you closer to freedom.

That lesson shows up in business all the time. Let me tell you about someone I met who learned it the hard way.

I was introduced to an entrepreneur a few years ago who, on paper, had pulled off the dream. He'd sold his business services company in a deal valued at $20 million. The announcement made headlines. And his peers celebrated him.

But when we met, it wasn't at a celebratory dinner…it was because he was looking for a job.

He shared what had happened. While the company *was* valued at $20 million, the deal was structured with only 10% of the payment made at closing. The rest tied to a non-guaranteed earnout. After taxes, splitting the upfront payment with his partner, and paying his advisors, he had very little actual cash in hand.

And when the acquisition didn't perform as projected, the private equity firm restructured everything. The earnout vanished. What the entrepreneur thought was a life-changing deal turned out to be nothing more than paperwork.

We talked for a while, and one thing stuck with me: he was never really clear on what mattered most to him. Was it the ego of a big headline number, or was it the real cash, the freedom, the security? He'd never defined success on his terms. And it cost him.

The scoreboard that matters isn't public.
It's personal.

From Entrepreneurial Poverty to Strategic Wealth

A study by the Small Business Administration found that 83% of small businesses, defined as those producing less than $25 million in annual revenue, which is anything but small, operate in a state of survival mode. They operate in an unsustainable pattern of closing a deal, spending the money, and then repeating the process.

Those 83% have limited profit. The owners of the businesses live deal to deal, year to year, and do not realize they have no hope of becoming the elite entrepreneurs that can fund a future, let alone have a sizable financial exit in their future.

You may have built a profitable business, but is it an asset you can step away from? To create a company that delivers true freedom: financial freedom, time freedom, and emotional freedom. You need to shift your focus to the right metrics:

- Profitability
- Efficiency
- Value

These numbers create long-term wealth and the possibility of an exit on your terms. And yet, most owners avoid this conversation.

Why? Because it's scary to talk about and prepare for our future. Not just dream about it.

So, what is a business?

It is a simple question that has become a complicated answer. Ask ten business owners, and you'll get ten different answers.

We treat business owners as leaders, community organizers, mentors, political influencers, and celebrities. Today's culture has defined business and business owners as all these things and more.

But in all the noise, we have lost sight of what a business truly is. Oxford Languages defines a business as "the practice of making one's living by engaging in commerce." You need to make a living to have a business.

Let's set the record straight: **"Profit" isn't a dirty word. Neither is "Value."**

Without profit, your business can't fulfill any missions. Without value, your business won't survive beyond you.

Most owners miss the critical piece: profitability is only one part of the equation. If you are stuck in the day-to-day operations of your business, even with a highly profitable business, your business is not a valuable asset; it's a dependency.

You've probably heard the concept of working *on* your business, rather than *in* it. Michael Gerber most extensively explores this concept in his book, *The E-Myth Revisited*. Michael says, "If your business depends on you, you don't own a business, you have a job. And it's the worst job in the world because you're working for a lunatic!"

The truth of the matter is that a lot of us live in the day-to-day. We claim to be working *on* our business or striving to do so, but when the pressure is on, we spend the bulk of our 9-to-5 hours buried in operations. We're the bottleneck. The firefighter. The answer to every question.

Why?

Because becoming an owner instead of an operator doesn't happen automatically. There's no magical switch that flips on some mythical day when the business stops needing you. It's like expecting to retire with a full 401(k) without ever saving a dime. It doesn't happen that way!

The same is true with building a valuable organization. It's a process that takes strategic effort over time to achieve. **It's not easy, but it's simple**. And the good news is that I will provide you with a simple path to freedom in the coming chapters. I've watched hundreds of business owners do it, and you can too.

Your Responsibility as a Business Owner

I grew up in Medford, New Jersey, a charming small town where I attended a large regional high school. (Go Renegades!) My graduating class consisted of approximately 600 students. However, now that I'm an entrepreneur, I view those numbers differently.

According to a 2022 Global Entrepreneurship Monitor study, approximately 9% of Americans became business owners over the previous 3.5 years. Other estimates vary, ranging from 3% to 19%, but 9–10% seems to be the sweet spot. If I apply that to my graduating class, that means maybe 54 of us went on to start businesses.

Now, here's where things get even more interesting. Of those 54 business owners, 8 out of 10 will run solo-preneur ventures, companies with no employees. That leaves just a handful, perhaps 10, who built businesses with employees. And of those, only about 13% are expected to achieve long-term success with a smooth exit transition. When you do the math, just five of us are responsible for employing others and sustaining those jobs long-term.

It's an incredible privilege but also an enormous responsibility.

Not just for your future but for the futures of everyone connected to your business. As your business grows larger, so does the responsibility.

This is your chance to leave a lasting legacy. You are not just running a business; you are affecting lives and building something that genuinely matters, whether you believe in it or not.

It's Time to Shift to Value Growth

So, it's time to shift your focus.

The real purpose is to create a return on our precious money and time investment. The accurate measure of the health of your company is its value.

Shifting your thinking to value is not just about numbers on a balance sheet; it's about reclaiming your role as a business owner and investor. You're building a business that thrives without your constant input and becomes an asset that can fund your dreams, support your family, and inspire your team.

You can step out of the endless cycle of doing and into the higher calling of creating. Let this be the moment you choose to focus on what matters most. You are not ordinary. You redefine what extraordinary looks like. And that starts with building a business of value.

- Value is the ultimate measure of success.
- Value creates a long-term legacy.
- Value sets you free.

So, value is the key metric by which we will now measure our business health. It's a holistic concept encompassing various elements, such as:

- Brand reputation
- Customer loyalty
- Operational efficiency
- Intellectual property
- Potential for future growth

A business with high value is resilient, adaptable, and attractive to potential buyers, investors, and partners. It can weather economic downturns, attract top talent, and command premium prices when it's time for the owner to exit.

The value of a company is primarily determined by its earnings. I go into much greater depth on valuation methods and formulas in my first book, *Getting the Most for Selling Your Business*, but here's a quick summary:

Small and mid-sized companies are valued at a multiple of their earnings. Earnings, which are defined as:

EBITDA	SDE
Earnings before Interest, Taxes, Depreciation, and Amortization	Seller's Discretionary Earnings: EBITDA + 1 Working Owner's Salary and Defined Benefits

These are the gold standard for business valuations, accepted by investment bankers, business acquirers, and, most importantly, lenders.

- A business is not valued based on its potential but on its historical performance.
- A business is only worth what an acquirer can afford based on actual cash flow.

Therefore, to be valuable, a business must be profitable (what I refer to as the quantitative aspect). That's the baseline, and we will extensively cover how to become wildly profitable in Chapter 5: Optimize Your Financials.

But profitability is just half of the puzzle. The second piece is the multiple. It's not true that there's a fixed multiple for your industry. Every industry has a range of multiples depending on the size and quality of the business. Multiples vary wildly, even within the same industry. So what makes one company worth 1x and another 25x? That's what we'll cover in the following chapters.

We will address both sides of the value equation, quantitative and qualitative, in this book, and together we will build a company that provides you, as an owner, a return on investment:

- A return on your money
- A return on your time
- A return on your risk

Case Study: Real Results from Value-Growth Thinking

This shift in mindset, from chasing revenue to building value, isn't just theory. It's real. And Joanne and Steve are living proof.

When they launched their medical device practice together over a decade ago, they had big dreams and endless energy. But by the time we connected, they were worn out. While successful on paper, their business had become a constant source of stress.

Despite having a skilled and dedicated team, every major decision and responsibility ultimately landed on their shoulders. They relied heavily on one large customer, whose inconsistent budgets sent their revenue on a frustrating roller coaster. It felt like they were stuck in a cycle of chaos, constantly asking, **"When will this get easier?"**

They realized they needed a change, not just for their business but for their lives. They had spent most of their life working, missing family events, vacations, and their kids' sports events. They would not repeat that mistake with their next shot, their grandchildren.

That's when they discovered the VORTEx Model, and everything shifted. With guidance, Joanne and Steve created a clear and exciting vision for the future. They defined their ultimate exit goal and took the necessary steps to achieve it.

First, they optimized their business's financial health, streamlining operations and diversifying their client base to reduce risk. Next, they tackled delegation, something that initially felt impossible. But as they trusted their team and gave them room to step up, something unexpected happened: they fell in love with their business all over again.

This renewed energy sparked growth they hadn't imagined. So when the perfect offer came along, they were ready, and because the business no longer depended on them, the transition was smooth and quick.

Within eighteen months, they increased the company's valuation by 89%, a rise worth $650,000. That extra equity gave them the freedom to retire early, pay off their home, and fund the future they'd dreamed of for their grandkids.

The best part? They only stayed on for a few months after the sale. The business no longer needed them, as they had followed a proven plan to build a company that could thrive without their involvement.

It wasn't luck. It was the result of following the VORTEx model step by step with expert guidance. And they'll be the first to tell you: "It was the best investment we ever made."

You Can't Exit What You Can't Escape

The reality is this: We aren't creating bad businesses, far from it. Sixty-five percent of companies are profitable. That is a VERY high number. The problem is that most of us are poor operators and business owners. But that is okay!

You probably didn't get into business because you are a naturally talented entrepreneur. You got into business because you were a great technician: a construction manager, technology developer, personal trainer, accountant, or (name any other trade you want). You may be great at what you do, but now you must learn how to become a great entrepreneur.

To truly thrive, we must make a conscious decision to adopt Value-Growth Thinking today, not years from now. Far too many of us delay our exit planning, assuming we will have time to sort it out later. I call this the **"Rolling Five."** At any given time, if I ask you how far out your exit is, you will probably tell me five years. If I ask you the same question next year, what do you think the answer will be? You got it, five years.

This approach of punting the ball down the field and putting off the critical task of preparing for the business's (and your) long-term future is a recipe for disappointment and missed opportunities.

A successful exit requires long-term preparation and consistent effort, **starting now**.

Your challenge is the same one faced by every business owner who has ever felt stuck: break away from the more than 80% who survive in chaos mode and join the Elite 13% who successfully exit their businesses with a financial return and set their company up for a long-term legacy. That requires a pledge to shift focus from immediate gains to long-term value creation. If you're willing, you can ensure that your business will support you in the short term and provide lasting value for years.

But before you begin working on the business, you need to start with your identity as a business owner. In the next chapter, I'll walk through the three stages every entrepreneur must evolve through if they want to build a business that works without them.

Your Move

Reflection
Take a moment to identify the mindset that's driving your decisions. Are you chasing "more" because it feels like progress, or are you truly building value?

Simple Action Step
Take the pledge to join the **Elite 13**, a group of business owners dedicated to building valuable businesses that are not just suited well for exit but for the ability to last a lifetime and beyond. Join our free community at exitfactorbook.com.

Tool to Use
Download the **Exit Factor Tool Kit for the remainder of this book** at exitfactorbook.com.

Chapter 2

THE THREE STAGES OF THE ENTREPRENEUR

Founder – Builder – Investor

Where do you go to learn how to be a business owner?

If you're anything like me, or the thousands of entrepreneurs I've worked with, you didn't go to school for this. You didn't get a manual. You learned by doing: through trial, error, and many long nights. You started your company because you were good at something and wanted more control, more income, or maybe just more freedom than a traditional job could offer.

But building a business is more than just launching a product or growing a team. The real challenge? Evolving *yourself* along the way.

The secret most books won't tell you?

Exit isn't just something your business goes through. It's something you personally go through as well.

Most entrepreneurs consider exit a final event, a transaction when you're ready to walk away. But it's not an event. Exit is a *phase*. Like startup and growth, it requires intention, preparation, and a different way of thinking.

I've learned that it's not just the *business* that evolves through stages. It's the *entrepreneur*.

Over time, every business owner must make three critical identity shifts:

- From the **Founder** (who does everything),
- To the **Builder** (who drives growth),
- To an **Investor** (who builds an asset that works without them).

When you reach that third stage, you are ready to build a valuable business.

Let's take a closer look at these three stages of entrepreneurial evolution because your business can't become a high-value asset unless *you* evolve alongside it.

Stage One: The Founder

Every business starts with a spark: a big idea, a moment of courage, or a breaking point where you say, "I can't do this job anymore. I need to build something of my own."

Welcome to the **Founder** stage.

This stage is where every entrepreneur begins: chasing an idea, doing everything themselves, and running on sheer energy and determination. You are the business. Your ideas, your time, your decisions. In this stage, it's all hustle, heart, and high-stakes improvisation.

It's scrappy. It's reactive. And it's exhilarating, for a while.

In this stage, you're not just the CEO. You're also the salesperson, the marketing team, the bookkeeper, the customer service rep, and the janitor. You're figuring out pricing while updating your website at midnight and sending invoices between client calls. If there's a decision to be made, a fire to put out, or a task that needs doing, it lands on your desk.

The identity of the Founder is: you *are* the business. And that's both the strength and the trap of this stage.

Believing "More" Will Fix It

The common belief at this stage? "More" will fix everything. More clients. More sales. More time spent grinding. If you just get a few more wins, you tell yourself, the pressure will ease. You'll catch up. You'll hire help. You'll figure out the rest.

But here's the catch: more work doesn't equal more value.

You can be the hardest-working Founder on the planet, but if everything still relies on you, you haven't built a business…you've built a job. And often, it's one of the worst jobs you've ever had. Because you're working *for a boss who doesn't know how to let go* (hint: it's you).

Many entrepreneurs get stuck here. They confuse activity with momentum. They chase growth but don't stop to build infrastructure. They want freedom but won't delegate. And over time, the initial excitement gives way to exhaustion.

The longer you stay in this stage, the more likely burnout becomes. Because eventually, there's just not enough of you to go around.

Most business books portray the startup stage as the thrilling beginning, often likening it to the garage story. However, the truth is that staying in this stage for too long becomes dangerous.

If everything your business needs to run lives in your head, then guess what? It can't run without you. And that means it can't scale, and you certainly can't exit.

Your business needs to evolve. But more importantly, *you* need to evolve. That's the only way to move forward.

When It's Time to Shift

You know it's time to shift out of the Founder stage when:

- You're drowning in decisions only you can make.
- You're exhausted but can't stop.
- You've hit a revenue ceiling you can't break without help.
- You dream about a vacation, but you can't imagine your business surviving one.

Sound familiar? Don't worry, you're not behind. This realization marks the turning point.

Once you recognize the limitations of this stage, you can begin the transition to the next: **The Builder**, where you stop being the business and start building something that works beyond you.

Stage Two: The Builder

You made it through the early chaos. You have paying clients, a working offer, and a team. You're no longer just a Founder, you're a Builder now.

This stage is the one where things start to feel real.

The company has legs. Your team is growing. You might even have an office, a logo that doesn't make you cringe, and systems that aren't just sticky notes on your desk. From the outside, you appear to be a success story.

But inside? You're still running hard.

Builders are ambitious. You're saying yes to new clients, new markets, and new team members. You're stacking revenue and dreaming about the next million. And that drive is a gift, but it's also a risk.

Because what got you through the Founder stage won't work here.

In this stage, the hustle becomes heavier. Your team needs leadership. Your clients want consistency. And your systems, if you have any, start to crack under the weight of new volume.

This stage is where growth can become a value trap.

Here's where many Builders get stuck: they think revenue will solve their problems. Just a little more. One big contract. A new product line. However, what they often build is a bloated business, not a better one.

You don't just need *more*…you need *margin*. You need clean operations, clear roles, and scalable processes. Without those, growth creates mass, not momentum.

Significant revenue is exciting. But *unprofitable* growth? It's a slow, expensive way to stall your exit.

Let me tell you about one of the clearest examples I've seen.

When Big Clients Break the Business

We once worked with a boutique software development firm that was determined to achieve growth. On the outside, they were crushing it with big-name Fortune 500 clients.

In their quest to land those marquee accounts, however, they cut their margins to win the deals. At first, those logos on the client list felt like gold. They told themselves that once the big names were in the door, the profits would follow. Spoiler: they didn't.

Those enterprise projects ultimately proved to be more demanding than profitable. Long timelines. Scope creep. Constant change orders. And the kicker? They had to pull their best developers off other, more profitable accounts just to keep up with the demands of these "trophy clients."

By the time we started talking, they wanted out, but the high revenue that looked so good on paper was dragging down their valuation. Buyers saw through the top line to the razor-thin margins with no scalable structure.

What appeared to be a success from the outside turned out to be one of the biggest value traps we've seen.

It's a perfect reminder that top-line growth means nothing if it's not profitable and sustainable.

The hidden truth about the Builder stage is that you're still at the center of everything.

Yes, you have a team. But you're still the one they look to for every major decision. You're still the one handling the most significant client issues, jumping onto sales calls, managing cash flow, and reviewing the final proposals.

It's growth, but it's not freedom.

And while you may feel successful, your business is still heavily dependent on you. Which means it's still not truly *valuable* in the eyes of a buyer.

To truly evolve into an Investor, you need to stop building a business around your talents and start building one that runs on systems, people, and processes.

That means letting go of:

- The idea that no one can do it like you.
- The belief that revenue equals health.
- The reflex to jump in and save the day.

Instead, you need to invest in your leadership team. Clean up your financials. Install real systems. Start measuring success not by how busy you are, but by how little the business needs you to function.

When It's Time to Shift

You're ready to leave the Builder stage when:

- Your revenue is substantial, but your profit is weak.
- You've hired a team, but you're still the bottleneck.
- Growth feels more exhausting than exciting.
- You're making more money, but you have even less freedom.

Sound familiar? That's your cue to step into Phase Three: the **Investor**, where your business becomes an asset, not just a job.

Stage Three: The Investor

If the Founder stage is about hustle and the Builder stage is about growth, the Investor stage is about *leverage.*

This stage is where your identity as a business owner undergoes its final evolution: from being the driver of the business…to being its strategist and steward. You're no longer the one pushing every wheel forward; you're designing the machine.

The goal in this stage is to transform your business from something that *depends on you* to something that can *outlive you.*

Because the truth is, you can't sell a job. You can only sell a business.

Investors look at their company differently than Founders or Builders. They ask different questions:

- How transferable is this company without me?
- How does each decision impact EBITDA?
- Where is our value trapped, and how do we unlock it?

You stop focusing solely on *sales* or *headcount growth* and start evaluating *risk*, *profitability*, and *operational independence*. You trade ego metrics for exit metrics.

At this stage, your goal is to make the business both *valuable* and *buyable*, which requires a clean break from how you've likely operated until now.

Let's be clear: the most valuable companies don't run on the charisma or brilliance of one person. They run on repeatable systems, well-trained teams, and documented knowledge.

Investors know this. That's why they:

- Delegate key responsibilities to a leadership team.
- Systematize their operations.
- Remove themselves from sales and client relationships.
- Make decisions that prioritize long-term value over short-term control.

You may still set the vision, but you're no longer the only one who can make it real.

The Power of Transferability

Transferability is your secret weapon. It's what turns a "nice business" into a valuable asset. It's also what allows you to step away: whether you plan to exit now, in five years, or not at all.
When your business can run (and grow) without you, you gain leverage, options, and freedom.

Let me give you an example of how transformational this can be.

Case Study: The Security Firm's Wake-Up Call

One of our Exit Factor clients, a successful security consulting firm, was run by two partners. Talented, driven, and seven years deep into the business, they had built a strong reputation and a solid book of business. But the model was entirely dependent on them.

During one of their annual retreats, they paused for the first time to ask the fundamental questions:

What kind of business are we building? Do we want to do this forever?

The answer was clear: **no**. Their dream was to exit in five to seven years, not grind it out for another fifteen or twenty. However, when we assessed the business, we saw the problem: they had built something successful, but not *something they could exit*. It was high-touch, deeply customized, and heavily reliant on their involvement.

The good news? They had already begun exploring a more scalable approach: productizing a piece of their expertise.

So, they pivoted the entire model.

We helped the owners redesign the business from the ground up, transforming it from a consulting practice into a scalable, systems-driven platform. They committed fully to the product side, reinvesting time, energy, and capital into building something they could eventually exit from.

The result? Not only did they align their company with their personal goals, but they also moved from an average valuation range of **3–7 times earnings** into a premium category, **10–20 times**.

They weren't even finished executing the entire plan when offers started coming in. Multiple buyers approached them with offers 500% higher than their original valuation. Why? Because the new model was **transferable**. It didn't require the founders to deliver the work. It could grow without them.

Let's break it down:

- If you're still running day-to-day sales, managing the team, and approving every invoice, you'll need a unicorn buyer to replace you.
- But if you've built a company where others lead, systems support the work, and knowledge is documented? Suddenly, you've got a hundred buyers. Maybe even more.

More buyers mean more competition, which in turn leads to more value.

Even if you don't plan to sell today, building a business that *can* sell is how you protect your wealth and your legacy.

Here's the most significant emotional shift that happens in this stage: you stop building a business to survive and start shaping it for life beyond you.

You can sell it. Scale it. Step back and collect dividends. Hand it off to someone else, or hold onto it and build an empire. But all of those options only exist when your company doesn't need you in the center.

One of the best examples of this is Sara Blakely. She didn't just build Spanx to be successful; she built it to operate without her. By the time she sold it for over $1 billion, she was spending most of her time on product design rather than operations. Her leadership team ran the company. The systems were dialed. And she retained complete control until she chose to let go.

That's what Investor thinking makes possible.

When You Know You're Ready

You've entered the Investor stage when:

- The business can run profitably without your daily involvement.
- Your team can make decisions without your sign-off.
- You have clean financials, defined processes, and documented roles.
- You're evaluating the company the same way a buyer would.

Most importantly, you no longer see yourself as *the business*. You know the company is a *financial asset*, one that can deliver wealth, legacy, and freedom.

Exit Doesn't Always Mean "Sell"

Now that you're thinking like an Investor, it's worth saying out loud:

> **Exiting your company doesn't always mean selling your company.**

Yes, selling is the most talked-about path, and I wrote the book on how to do it right (*Getting the Most for Selling Your Business*). But it's not the only option.

The true power of reaching this stage is that **you now have options available to you.** Let's break them down.

Your Exit Options

OPTION	WHAT IT MEANS	PROS / CONS
Selling to a Third Party	Outside buyer: a competitor, private equity firm, search fund, or a company going public	+ Highest potential payout − Most complex
Transitioning to the Next Generation	Selling or gifting to a family member or business partner	+ Legacy play − Personal dynamics matter
Employee Ownership	Selling to your team through a structured buyout	+ Strong continuity and culture − Complex setup and financing
Hiring a CEO	Stepping back and collecting dividends	+ Keeps income flowing − Requires strong leadership and systems
Orderly Dissolution	Closing the doors, liquidating, and walking away	+ Sometimes the cleanest choice − Emotionally challenging, lowest financial outcome

You don't need to pick your final path today (we'll do that later in Chapter 8). However, it's worth considering which of these *could* align with your personal, financial, and lifestyle goals. Which ones feel exciting? Which ones feel impossible (for now)?

When Is It Time to Exit?

A question I hear frequently is, *"How do I know when it's time to move on?"*

The best answer is this: keep one toe in the exit box at all times. That means running an annual Exit Assessment on your business and asking yourself two essential questions:

1. Do I have the time to execute this roadmap?
2. Do I have the energy to execute this roadmap?

If the answer to either question is no, it may be time.

The point isn't to rush toward an exit. It's to *build the option*. And that starts by stepping fully into the Investor role. Because when you do that, you don't have to wait for burnout, a health scare, or a surprise offer. You can exit on your terms with clarity, leverage, and control.

The Journey Isn't Linear, But It Can Be Intentional

Founder. Builder. Investor. These aren't rigid steps. You may move forward, then back. You may rebuild parts of your foundation before you can scale again.

But when you understand where you are and what's next, you can make smarter decisions. You can exit from a place of strength, not survival.

Now that we have adopted the value-growth mindset and understand that to evolve our business, we must evolve ourselves, we are ready to begin the real work. In the next chapter, we'll walk through the VORTEx Model: a framework designed to help you align your strategy, streamline your systems, and prepare your business (and yourself) for whatever comes next.

Your Move

What Stage Are You In?

You've just read about the three stages of the entrepreneurial journey: the Founder, Builder, and Investor. Now it's time to get honest about where you are right now.

This quiz isn't a pass/fail test. It's a quick gut check to help you take the next right step in your business journey and start thinking like someone who's building toward value.

Grab a pen. Select the box that most closely aligns with your current experience. Be brutally honest; your future self will thank you.

1. **Your Role Today**
   A. I do almost everything myself.
   B. I've hired a few people, but I'm still the final word on most things.
   C. My team handles day-to-day operations, and I primarily focus on strategy, vision, and investments.

2: Your Time

A. I work constantly, and I can't remember the last time I truly unplugged.
B. I'm still very involved, but I've started carving out space for other priorities.
C. I can be away from the business for weeks, and it continues to run smoothly.

3: Your Financials
   A. I'm focused on generating revenue and staying afloat.
   B. We're growing, but profitability is inconsistent or low.
   C. We track EBITDA, manage margins, and forecast our value with confidence.

4: Your Systems
   A. What systems? Most things live in my head.
   B. We have some documented processes, but I still fill in the gaps.
   C. We have clear systems, roles, and SOPs—and I'm not the bottleneck.

5: Your Exit Readiness
- A. Exit? I'm too busy surviving to think about that.
- B. I've thought about it, but the business relies on me too much.
- C. I already have serious offers from multiple buyers.

Results:

Mostly A's: You're in the Founder stage.
You're building something from the ground up. Right now, it's all about survival, hustle, and wearing all the hats. Your goal? Start thinking of your business as a system, rather than an extension of yourself.

Mostly B's: You're in the Builder stage.
You've got traction and a team. Now, the challenge is scaling smart, not just fast. Your goal is to focus on the financial return that the business is providing you while also removing yourself as the bottleneck.

Mostly C's: You're in the Investor stage.
You're thinking like a strategist, and you've built something that can run without you. Now it's time to sharpen efficiency, boost value, and plan your ideal exit on your terms.

SECTION TWO

PREPARING YOUR COMPANY

Chapter 3

THE VORTEX MODEL

Your Roadmap to Exit Readiness

No matter where you are in your business or as an entrepreneur, it's worth saying this: you should always run your business like you are going to exit it. But that doesn't mean abandoning the growth that you still want to achieve. There is a model that you can take your business through to ensure that you can exit at any time for maximum value. And, if you choose to keep it, it provides you with the time, money, and freedom you desire as an owner.

That model is called the VORTEx.

You Can't Start a Fire Without a Spark

As a child, my parents hoped for anything but an entrepreneur. I grew up in a family where "safe and secure" was the mantra. My mom was a nurse, and my dad worked in education. They had great benefits, solid pensions, and a firm belief that the best path forward was a stable corporate job.

But like many stories, there's a twist.

Entrepreneurship *ran* in my blood. My great-great-grandfather was a bootlegger. My great-grandfather owned bars. And my grandfather ran a successful chain of pharmacies until it all came crashing down.

He worked himself to the bone, missed countless family moments, and when the big chains like CVS and Eckerd swept in, he had no plan. He sold for pennies, and the family had to start over from scratch. My dad stepped in to support my grandmother and vowed that things would be different for us.

And they were. My parents never missed a game, a recital, or a school event. They advised me to secure a stable job with a 401(k) and excellent benefits.

So, you can imagine the horror on my dad's face when I decided to start my business during the 2007–08 financial crisis. I had no roadmap. No generational wealth. No mentor. Just hustle, grit, and a wine shop because someone had to carry on the family theme of booze and drugs! I was determined to control my future and build a business I could be proud of.

And it grew fast.

By 2012, we were thriving. We had fallen into a very niche area of the wine industry, working with collectors and specialty buyers selling wine priced between $500 and $25,000 a bottle (yes, there really is wine that expensive in the world). To outside eyes, the business was a huge success. Behind the scenes? I was working beyond exhaustion. Between retail store hours and clients on three different continents, it was a pace I couldn't keep up.

I cracked one ordinary morning when I had a blow dryer in my hand. I called my mom, sobbing, not about the hair, but everything it represented. She gently said what I didn't want to hear: *"Maybe it's time to take a break."*

I listened. I flew to Aspen, unplugged, and let myself breathe. And somewhere between a run on Back of Bell and après champagne, the truth hit me: *I didn't want this anymore.*

Not the business. Not the hours. Not the life I'd created.

So I turned to my husband and said, *"I need to sell."*

That moment changed everything. But for all the resources out there about starting and scaling a business, *no one* prepares you for how to leave one. I was left scrambling with no real guidance, just vague advice, a mediocre broker, and Google.

That was the moment I realized that exits don't just happen. They have to be built.

Somehow, we closed the deal. But it could've gone sideways at any moment. And I couldn't stop thinking: If I nearly failed, with a profitable and well-run company, how many others are walking into their exits completely unprepared?

Why Exit Factor Exists

That question lit the fire.

I was inspired to serve business owners that no one else was serving, real entrepreneurs running companies with under $50 million in revenue. Too small for Wall Street, but also too successful to walk away without a plan.

So, I built the system I wish I'd had.

I started a new company focused on mergers and acquisitions advisory services and quickly grew, expanding to four states, and eventually adding the Exit Factor division, which helps entrepreneurs prepare for a future exit. At the time of this writing, Exit Factor now has franchises throughout the United States. It has been recognized by some of the top publications for our innovative but simple model and our success rates.

But the real win isn't the growth or the awards. It's what we've learned from helping thousands of business owners navigate the most critical moment of their entrepreneurial journey: the exit.

As we discussed in the first chapter, many entrepreneurs are stuck in a cycle of burnout, hoping the next big deal will be their ticket out. Many owners think they're building a "legacy" business: something to pass on, or a monument to their hard work.

But legacy is often an ego trap. What you want is optionality: the ability to sell, scale back, or step away on your terms.

Introducing the VORTEx Model

The Exit Factor program is a proven method designed to provide business owners with three key benefits: **time, money, and freedom**.

At its heart is the VORTEx Model. This framework helps you build a profitable and valuable company today, positioning you for a successful exit tomorrow. Like a tornado, the VORTEx Model gets its power from the top, building a solid business model and foundation. Then, when we are ready, we narrow your focus, build energy, and channel it toward one powerful moment: your exit.

Let's break it down phase by phase so you can apply it to your business.

VORTEx stands for:

- Value – Define your exit goals and understand what your business is worth.
- Optimize – Get your financials in shape and maximize profitability.
- Record – Systematize operations and reduce owner-dependence.
- Transform – Grow intentionally, strategically, and profitably.
- Exit – Craft and execute a plan that aligns with your goals and sets you up for life after your business.

A VORTEx Success Story: Marcus's Strategic Exit

Marcus built a successful commercial cleaning company serving mid-sized office complexes and industrial facilities.

After years of long hours and growing a reputable brand, he knew he was ready to move on. But he didn't want to walk away with regret or leave money on the table.

So, he did what few business owners have the discipline to do: he started preparing early. Over two years, Marcus worked through every phase of the VORTEx framework.

- In **Value**, he clarified his ideal timeline, goals, and exit priorities.
- In **Optimize**, he restructured his pricing, cut low-margin contracts, and improved net profit across his top five clients.
- In **Record**, we helped him document service procedures, train a second-in-command, and ensure that clients weren't relying solely on him.
- In **Transform**, Marcus leaned into a targeted growth strategy by offering bundled maintenance packages, boosting contract size without adding operational complexity.
- Then, in **Exit**, he took his business to market.

The outcome? His company experienced an 80% increase in value over the two years. When it sold, he walked away with over $600,000 more than he would've without that preparation. And the icing on the cake? No seller financing. No long-term earnout. He was fully transitioned out within sixty days.

Now, Marcus is onto his next chapter, fully exited, fully paid, and entirely in control of what's next.

When you exit right, you create an impact that ripples beyond the transaction.

Following the VORTEx Model doesn't just create exit readiness, it creates peace of mind.

Whether you plan to sell today, plan to sell in the future, or want to step back and let someone else lead, one thing is sure: *you will exit your business someday.* The only question is, *will you be ready?*

The Three Outcomes of Exit Factor

There are numerous business operational systems available, but this is not one of them. The Exit Factor program with our VORTEx Model is a method of running a business to ensure that you, as an owner, have three things:

- **Time** – To focus on what matters most, in and outside your business.
- **Money** – A business that pays you now and builds wealth for later.
- **Freedom** – The power to exit when you want, on your terms.

Time

I recently saw a social media post that glorified overworked entrepreneurs. The text said, "People complain they have a full-time workload and don't have enough time to improve or grow their business. What are you doing with your weekends?"

I don't know about you, but I have more important things on my plate on the weekends and evenings than spending more time working on or in my business. I create lasting memories with my son, deepen my relationship with my spouse, spend quality time with my sisters and parents, and even just rest, allowing my body and brain to recover.

One of my friends says all the time, '*No one on their deathbed wishes they had worked more.*' And it's true. You don't need to work more; you need to work smarter. You need to make time work for you instead of repeatedly investing more time into fixing the same problems.

Money

Investing your money and time in a business is risky! We just read about how many business owners fail to launch, fail to scale, and fail to exit. The people who take on this journey of entrepreneurship must be truly insane! Compounding that stress is the financial pressure.

When I was growing up, I thought every business owner was wealthy and successful (my dad didn't share my family's history with me until much later in life). And much of the general public thinks like I did. But we know the myth that all entrepreneurs are wealthy couldn't be further from the truth; often, they are making less than they would at a job and have the debt to back it up.

Running a business that doesn't generate a profit is stressful. And that stress, slowly and then suddenly, gives way to burnout, the number one reason entrepreneurs give up on their businesses. As we learned, giving up on our businesses doesn't just impact us but everyone and everything around us. The problem is not that you care too much; you've built something that isn't paying you back.

We NEED you to make enough money not just to survive, but also to have a thriving personal financial life that makes all the stress and risk worthwhile. There has to be gold at the end of this rainbow.

Freedom

I talk a lot about exits. Even if that is not the immediate plan, I don't want this program and this book to lose you. This process is about building value so you can exit on your terms, not because you're forced to. You will have many choices if you design a company with a value-growth mindset.

- Do you want to exit?
- When do you want to exit?
- Which method of exit do you prefer?
- And, what is your role after the exit?

When your business is valuable, you get the freedom to choose. So that's our goal: time, money, and freedom.

But most business owners wait too long to take action and prepare for their exit. The reason for it? They don't know where to start.

The Five Phases of the VORTEx Model

When deciding on the proper model to help business owners achieve their future goals, I searched for the strategies and tactics that are the most critical to running a great company today while preparing for an exit in the future.

If you are like me, you already have enough on your plate. Managing employees, serving clients, and keeping up with the ever-changing business landscape is enough. I don't need to add hours of meetings, days of planning, and complex tracking systems to your plate to tell you what you already know…your business isn't giving you what you need.

After researching and learning from some of the top programs and minds, from Tony Robbins to MIT, and testing it on my businesses and those of my clients, I developed this simple toolset to ensure that we build businesses that make our lives simpler and better.

That's what the VORTEx Model is. The Exit Factor program focuses on five key phases. While you can complete them in any order, we suggest working on them sequentially because they build on each other and create momentum.

The five phases of the VORTEx Model are:

Phase 1: Value – Know Your Destination

The primary reason entrepreneurs fail in their final exit is that they are unclear about their goals and how those goals align with market expectations.

It's funny, right? We spend a significant amount of time setting business goals, often centered around surface-level metrics. Things like:

- Revenue
- Number of locations
- Team size

While all crucial indicators are important, none guarantee a successful or profitable exit. But we spend little to no time or research pondering our business's final outcomes:

- What do you want out of your business, both now and later?
- Do you need to sell to meet your personal financial goals?
- Do you even *know* your personal financial goals?
- What is your business worth today?
- (Hint: It's not what you heard at the latest industry conference or what that free online calculator said.)
- And what happens if your expectations don't match what the market is willing to pay?

That last question is the one that kills the deal for most business owners. It's a reality check. And most of us avoid it until it's too late.

What the Beatles Can Teach Us About Exit Strategy

Besides teaching me the value of hard work, the other lesson my parents imparted upon me was a respect for good music, primarily classic rock and roll. And while most people know me for my deep commitment to Bruce Springsteen, I follow and love many other bands, including the original Fab Four: The Beatles.

Believe it or not, the Beatles offer a masterclass in what **not** to do when exiting your business. They were the most iconic band in the world. But by the end of their run, things were falling apart behind the scenes. While the world spun the vinyls of *Let It Be*, the Beatles were unraveling, fighting over direction, control, finances, and who owned what.

Why? Because they never aligned on the end game.

They hadn't discussed what success looked like beyond fame. They never got clear on their roles, the future of the business, or how (or even *if*) they'd ever walk away. So, instead of exiting with intention, they fractured under the weight of their success. Personal tensions and business misalignment created a slow-motion breakup that left money, opportunity, and a lot of legacy drama on the table.

The Beatles' story might seem like rock and roll drama, but it's a mirror for many entrepreneurs. We focus on annual growth, celebrate revenue milestones, and get high on headcount. But in doing so, we often forget the most important questions:

What are we *building toward*?

And are we building in a way that someone else will want to buy it?

The failure of an entrepreneur on their final exit is not due to a lack of effort. It's a lack of **clarity**: clarity on goals, timing, financial needs, and whether those expectations align with market reality.

Even the best businesses fall apart without a clear exit vision.

Introducing The Value Vision Map

That's why **Phase 1: Value** is so significant. It starts with one essential tool: your **Value Vision Map** (VVM).

Here's what the Value Vision Map includes:

1. **Your inspiring future.** What do you want to be when you grow up? No, seriously, what is the point of this entire business? What do you want to get out of it, and what do you want to do next?
2. **Your top exit priorities.** Based on your inspiring future, do you need to focus on cash, legacy, or stability?
3. **Time to exit.** Use our reverse timeline tool to determine the optimal time to exit and when you should begin.
4. **Your ideal exit option.** Sell? Transition to family? Internal buyout? Hire a CEO and become an absentee owner? (We'll revisit this in Phase 5: Exit).
5. **A financial health check.** How does your business valuation stack up against where you need it to achieve your goals?

The Value Vision Map becomes your North Star. It's how we prevent a Beatles-style breakup and guide you toward a smooth, strategic, and *valuable* exit.

Now that we know where we are going, we must ensure we have the right financial model to get us there.

Phase 2: Optimize – Turn Your Numbers Into a Strategic Asset

In this phase, we turn your numbers into a strategic asset, but don't worry, this isn't a scary math class. The primary objective of **Phase 2: Optimize** is to ensure you're no longer intimidated by your business's financials, but instead, you feel in control of your numbers, perhaps for the first time.

Let's start by reframing how we think about numbers. Most business owners already use scorecards to track progress, including revenue, new sales leads, customer satisfaction, and marketing metrics.

But here's a surprise: your financial statements are just another scorecard. But this one? It carries the most weight. If you love your numbers, they will love you! Controlling your financial picture is not your controllers' or your accountants' job; it is your number one priority as an owner.

Your financials are what set the value of your business. Buyers rely on them to decide if your company is worth buying. And, they're what banks look at to determine if your business is stable and profitable enough to fund now and at your exit.

Put simply: **your numbers tell the story of your business.** And if the story is confusing, incomplete, or inconsistent, your exit options die.

Weak or disorganized financials are one of the top reasons deals fall apart. Even when an exit is successful, your financials determine how much **cash** you walk away with and how much you might have to leave behind in seller financing or earnouts.

In Phase 2, we roll up our sleeves and clean up our act. We're not just trying to boost your value; we're also aiming to get you the *most* profit **now** in your business. We achieve this by building financial confidence and discipline into your business, starting today.

The Profit Pulse Plan

One of the biggest tools we implement during Optimize is your **Profit Pulse Plan** (PPP).

This tool allows us to focus on the most essential items in your financials:

- **Target net profit percentage:** What is the bar (or minimum viable profit margin) your company needs? Along with this, we will establish other key financial metrics.
- **Waste or misuse:** Identify what expenses have gotten out of control or have been misused.
- **Plan for the future:** It's not enough to identify waste; we must devise a plan to obliterate it.
- **Rhythm moving forward:** Now that we have achieved a new profit bar, we establish how to increase momentum with a review cadence for the future, preventing expense creep from happening again.

By the end of this phase, you'll have a much clearer picture of what's *working* in your business, what's *wasting money*, and what's truly *necessary* for your growth. You'll also know when it's smart to invest and when to hold back.

That kind of clarity isn't just good for your exit. It's suitable for your life.

When your business is financially optimized, you create more profit today. That means more cash flow for your family, more breathing room in your budget, and more flexibility to invest in whatever matters most to you: hiring a new team member, buying real estate, or just taking that vacation you've been putting off.

And all the while, you're steadily building a business that someone else will one day pay millions to own.

Phase 3: Record – Get Out of the Weeds, Permanently

The phrase "working on the business, not in the business" is so played out for me. Yes, Michael Gerber (author of *E-Myth Revisited*, which popularized this concept) is a genius, but now every business advisor has jumped on the trend. The problem? No one ever gives you a clear path to do it! When you start your business, you are playing all of the roles. It's not like you wake up one day, think, *Hey, I'm going to start working **on the business***, and poof! All of the roles and responsibilities you have are gone.

But unlike most "get things off your plate" models, I have found a formula for getting yourself out of roles that increases the value of your company. Some roles you occupy as an owner are more valuable or risky than others. And when a new owner finally comes into your business, they'll have two big fears:

1. Will the customers leave when *you* leave?
2. Will the employees leave when *you* leave?

If the answer to either of those is "maybe," you've got a transferability problem. It's foundational to creating a company that can function without you. In the mergers and acquisitions (M&A) world, we refer to this as a semi-absentee or absentee-owner business. Companies like these often command **0.5 to 2 times higher multiples** than owner-operated ones.

In **Phase 3: Record**, we use one of the most powerful tools in the Exit Factor to make that happen: the **Role Release Roadmap**.

This tool helps identify what you should keep doing, automate what you can, delegate what you should, and eliminate anything that's not working.

Excellence but Efficiency

One of my greatest joys in life is good food. However, for some chefs, building a business is more akin to creating art, and art isn't easily transferable. Take Jiro Ono, the legendary sushi master from the documentary *Jiro Dreams of Sushi*. His tiny restaurant tucked inside a Tokyo subway station earned three Michelin stars and global acclaim, attracting celebrities and heads of state. But when it came time to hand the business over to his son, Jiro waited until late in life. His sushi? World-renowned. But his business? Small, concentrated, and dependent on him.

Now, compare that to one of my favorite chefs, José Andrés. He started in the U.S. in the 1990s, running Jaleo in Washington, D.C. As Andrés opened more restaurants, he trained his chefs and teams to deliver the same guest experience, whether he was in the kitchen or halfway across the world. Today, he has built over forty restaurants, earned Michelin stars, and expanded beyond his initial involvement. That freed him to launch World Central Kitchen, which has served over 500 million meals to communities affected by disaster, war, and famine.

> Jiro built a masterpiece and passed it to his son. Andrés built a movement. Both paths are valid. But only one happens when you embrace the delegation and elevation strategies we're unpacking in this book

Too many business owners fall into the trap of being "the only one" who can do certain things. The only one who can run payroll, smooth over operations issues, or pick the right vendors. Sound familiar?

The great businesses, the ones that are sellable and scalable, don't rely on the owner's brilliance. They operationalize that brilliance. They teach, train, and document it.

Phase 4: Transform – Grow Intentionally, Not Chaotically

By this point, you've already done the heavy lifting. You've defined your target. You've optimized your financials. You've removed yourself from the day-to-day operations. Now comes the part that most business owners *think* should come first, but when done right, actually comes fourth: **strategic growth**. This is the **Transform** phase of the VORTEx Model, where we go from tuning the engine to stepping on the gas.

For years, the dominant narrative in entrepreneurship has been "grow first, fix later." We've all heard the phrase "move fast and break things," but we're not in the business of breaking things; we're in the business of building value.

Growth will likely be necessary if you're targeting a 50% increase in the value of your business, or more. But not just any kind of growth. It's not growth that looks good on paper, but it drains your cash.

This phase focuses on growth that supports your bottom line first. If it grows your top line, too? Even better. But we never sacrifice profitability or operational stability just to add zeros to revenue.

The 3-Growth Matrix

How do we know which growth path is right for your business? That's where I introduce **the 3-Growth Matrix** (3GM).

This exercise helps you determine which strategic lever will move the needle most for your business:

1. **Customer Expansion Lever** – Deepen your understanding of your ideal customer to enable you to expand your reach and acquire more just like them.
2. **Product/Service Line Expansion Lever** – Increase value to your existing customers by expanding your offerings or packaging them in a new way.
3. **Acquisition Lever** – Purchase another business, team, or customer base to accelerate your path to exit.

Each lever comes with its risks and return potential. In the chapter on Transform, we'll break these down in detail and show you how to decide which one to pull based on your timeline, goals, and current strengths.

Phase 5: Exit—Make It Happen on Your Terms

Last, it's time for the final step, **Phase 5: Exit.** We'll revisit your goals from Phase 1: Value to help identify your best exit option, how to stage and position the business to attract the right buyer pool, and put the right team of advisors in place to ensure success.

For most entrepreneurs, the idea of leaving the business feels abstract or uncomfortable. It's easy to delay. It feels like you're either selling out or walking away. However, the truth is that your exit is not just a transaction. It's the moment when everything you've built finally pays off.

The problem? Most owners don't decide *how* to exit until they are forced. And by then, it's too late to shape the outcome. They end up stuck with options that don't reflect what they want or need, personally or financially.

Whether you want to exit in one year or five, clarity is a powerful asset. We'll define success for you and start building the path to get there.

How to Use This Book and Program

How you use this book and the Exit Factor program is entirely up to you. I wrote this book to meet you where you are, whether you're planning your exit next year or just beginning to think about the future.

Option 1: Do It Yourself

You can go through the program on your own. This book includes the tools, frameworks, and strategies you need to build a more profitable, efficient, and valuable business. If you'd like more structure or accountability, consider our companion course and community of business owners at your exact place at exitfactorbook.com. It's a great way to delve deeper into the material and connect with others who are walking the same path.

But let's be real: reading about strategy and doing the work are very different.

Option 2: Do It With Help

Sometimes you need someone in your corner. Just like you're the expert in your business, our certified Exit Factor consultants are experts in value growth and exit strategy. They're here to help you navigate the complexities, decisions, and emotions that come with stepping away from your business.

Each consultant is trained to guide business owners through their own customized journey of the VORTEx Model. Whether your plan involves selling, transitioning to a team member or family, or simply taking a step back, they help you design the path that fits *you*.

If you'd like to work one-on-one with a consultant, go to exitfactorbook.com, and we'll match you with the right person based on your goals, business, and timeline.

Block the Time. Protect the Time.

The time it takes to complete the program depends on your goals and your level of commitment. But here's what I recommend: **one hour per week**. That's it.

And here's the secret: our most successful clients don't just *hope* they'll find the time. They schedule it. They block it off and protect it as if it were a meeting with their biggest customer.

So do this now: open your calendar, create a recurring one-hour block, and label it "Exit Factor." That time is for you.

Use it to:

- Re-read or break down sections of this book.
- Complete the exercises in the book and on exitfactorbook.com.
- Meet with your consultant if you have one.

So, now you know where we're headed and why it matters. You've seen my story, the gap in the market that inspired this model, and the five phases that form the Exit Factor system. What comes next is the real work.

No more waiting until burned out, boxed in, or forced to move quickly. Let's start treating your exit as the goal and your business as the asset it is meant to be.

Now that we have a comprehensive overview of the VORTEx model, we will proceed to the most critical stage: Value. Even if you think you have your exit strategy dialed in, this is a can't-miss step. If we aren't 1,000% clear on the direction we are going, we may end up at the wrong destination.

Your Move

Reflection

Are you ready to run your business like an Investor with a disciplined approach?

Simple Action Step

Commit one hour per week. Our most successful clients don't give themselves another forty-hour-a-week job to implement the VORTEx Model; they schedule just one hour per week. Go to your calendar and commit that time right now. And if you don't have an hour? You need this more than you think.

Tool to Use

Download the **VORTEx Model** and the entire **Exit Factor Tool Kit for the remainder of this book** at exitfactorbook.com.

Chapter 4

PHASE 1: VALUE

Define What You Want and What It's Worth

*Build Your Value Vision Map and
Set Your Exit Direction*

Where We Are in the VORTEx

Welcome to Phase 1 of the Exit Factor program: **Value**, the foundation of everything that comes next.

Phase 1: Value

You know the saying: Begin with the end in mind. This single statement could not be more true in business. If you don't know where you are going with your exit, or when, you will never be able to design a plan on how to get there. For example, if you plan to sell your business in five years to maximize your cash at closing, it is very different from a plan to sell to your employees through an Employee Stock Ownership Plan (ESOP) in the next year.

And that is why we start with the Value you want to derive from your organization.

You've probably read books about how to start a business. Maybe a few on how to grow one. But what about the third act, the *exit*? Most owners ignore it until they are burned out, blindsided, or boxed in.

As we previously discussed, everyone exits. Feet first or head held high (until one of you savvy entrepreneurs figures out eternal life), we all go. However, the difference is that some of us will exit successfully through a sale or transition to employees or family, while others will have to close the doors. Your choice today is whether to control that future exit or let fate be the deciding factor. You can choose to ignore it or embrace it. The choice is yours.

Get The Resources from exitfactorbook.com
Before we proceed, please download the tools I reference throughout the remainder of the book. You can find them at exitfactorbook.com. If you'd like to review the book's content first, don't worry, I'll guide you through each step. However, the key to achieving fast momentum is taking action.

Why We Begin with the End in Mind

Now we get serious about what your business is worth, not just what your gut (or your friend's friend who knows someone in your industry) says it might be. By the end of this chapter, you'll walk away with a tool we call the **Value Vision Map**, your custom roadmap to the exit you want, not just the one you end up with by default.

You may remember the story I shared earlier about my grandfather, the one who built a successful chain of pharmacies, only to sell for pennies when the big players swept in.

He worked himself to the bone for that business. He didn't take many vacations, and he didn't make it to many of my dad's football games. And while that work ethic shaped my father, and by extension shaped me, there's a part of me that wonders how things might have been different if he'd had a plan.

Financially, sure. If he'd exited well, that sale might have changed the wealth trajectory of our entire family. But it's not just the money I think about. I wonder: Would he have been happier? Would he have had more peace in his later years? Would I have spent more time with him, not just as a grandfather but as a mentor?

That's what regret can look like, not dramatic failure, but missed potential.

This chapter is about making sure you don't end up with those same questions. That you don't just build a business but also craft the future you actually want for yourself, your family, and your legacy.

This exercise isn't about spreadsheets and snooze-worthy valuation formulas. Okay, there *are* a couple…but I promise they're spicy. These actions are about getting clear on five key things.

Phase 1: Value

The 5 Parts of the Value Vision Map
- Create your inspiring future.
- Identify your top exit priorities.
- Establish a timeline.
- Pick the ideal exit option.
- Make sure your finances support that vision.

An Inspiring Future – Design Your Life After Exit

So, what do you want to do when you grow up? No, seriously. If you're lucky, you only get a few chances in your life to design your future and your future self. It may seem a "soft" way to start a book on business exits, but this piece is critical to your success. According to a 2024 survey by the Exit Planning Institute, 75% of business owners report profound regret about exiting their companies.

Let that sink in. 75%...profoundly regret. Some reasons are that they left money on the table (that won't be you, now that you are committed to this program!), but most of them feel regret because they lack purpose once their business is gone.

I hated my first business. I wasn't passionate about wine or the industry. So when I sold the company, I never imagined I would mourn it. But I did.

Run Toward Something, Not Away From It

The reason I did? Because when I sold my company, I no longer played that role in life. And all of my daily activities and purpose were gone. That's why having an inspiring vision for your future is so important. You need something you run to, not just run away from. Ultimately, this vision for your future is your own; I can't help you craft it. However, I can offer you ideas from clients and friends who have successfully exited. Here are some to get you started:

- Start or buy another business that you are more passionate about.
- Get a job in an industry you love.
- Stay home and become a caretaker for a loved one—whether children, a parent, or a pet!
- Start or become involved in a charity.
- Reignite your career as a musician.
- Sail around the world.
- Travel with your children.
- Move to another country and build a bed and breakfast.
- Return to your home country and use your newfound wealth for good.
- Road trip across the United States, Europe, or Asia.
- Start a family.
- Re-engage with your family.
- Write a book (or a few).

Notice not one of them said, "retire" or "figure it out later." Additionally, none of them is a comprehensive life plan. You need a plan to get through the first year after your exit. I have found that having at least one year planned out will, first, help motivate you through the entire process of improving and exiting your business over the next few years, and second, prevent the profound regret we just learned about.

So, now it's your turn. Open your Value Vision Map and fill in Section 1. Complete the answers to help craft your inspiring future. I particularly enjoy the 'Describe Your Day' exercise. Whenever I feel stuck with envisioning my future, no matter what I'm planning, I do this exercise, and I can immediately see what I want.

For those of you following along with the Toolkit, please refer to your Value Vision Map and complete the answers to the questions in Step 1. They are repeated below for your reference, in case you are just reading along for now.

VVM Step 1: Inspiring Future Exercise

1. What do you want to do with your first year after exit?
2. Why is this important to you?
3. How will this provide meaning to your life?
4. Describe in detail a random day during that year.

Your Top Exit Priority—Know What Matters Most

Equally as crucial as exiting your business is doing so in a way that supports your core values. Each of us started our business for different reasons. That reason may be the same from the day we founded the company to today, or it may have morphed and changed.

Now, when considering our exit, our core values will significantly influence the exit we choose and how we execute it. One thing I want you to be aware of from the very beginning is your **most important outcome.** Each one of us will have one, and only one.

I never imagined myself in a career where sales and negotiation played such a key role in my life. In my early career working in the sports industry, I was allergic to sales. I ducked any negotiation, including my salary. But here I sit, as what some may consider an expert in the skill. And the number one thing I know about deals and negotiation is that **you can't win every battle.**

Like your grandmother said, you can't have your cake and eat it too. The exit that provides you with the most money? It may not be suitable for your employees. That legacy play where your kids take over? You may not get paid for a few years, or at all.

So, before we get into the heavy lifting of even picking what type of exit you want in the future, you need to know what's important to you.

The key outcomes you can choose from are:

1. **Money:** It's okay to pick money. To put your heart at ease, most of our clients (over 80%) opt for money. But it's not enough just to pick money. Do you want the highest *value* for your business or the most *cash* at close? Because they are not the same thing.
   - **Value:** The highest-valued deals typically require you to get paid over time through a seller's promissory note or an earnout. Meaning, you become the bank. These structures carry many risks, but they can also have good reasons and offer substantial rewards. We aren't going into all the details here, but I just want you to identify: is value, or the price you sell for, your most important outcome? Or is it…
   - **Cash:** The highest cash deals may not be the highest valuation. Often, receiving a substantial amount of money at exit means that the acquiring party is using outside financing. If that is the case, a lender will be involved, and wild valuations are out of the question, as lenders are limited by debt-to-income ratios.

2. **Legacy:** Or do you want to ensure that your business, and its culture, is passed on to caring hands? That may be the next generation of your family, employees, or even an outsider. If you select this option, you may leave money on the table or accept payment over time to achieve this.
3. **Your People:** Many owners want to ensure that their employees are taken care of. This could be in the form of job security or a payout on the sale. If your people are your priority, that may eliminate some exit options or buyers, and even mean you receive a lower payout for the company.
4. **A Place for You:** Some owners no longer want to be the leader. They want to stay on in the business because they feel like they have taken it as far as it can go. But this does not mean they want to leave! Maintaining a job for yourself or transitioning into the next growth cycle can be your primary outcome.
5. **Sail Off Into the Sunset:** This is the "leave me alone" priority. Every exit will require a transition in the form of you helping train the new leader on how to run the company (although this will be drastically reduced if you complete this program). But some owners are just DONE. They will leave money on the table and overlook the business's legacy, all in the name of being able to walk away *quickly*.

So, what is your most important outcome? Write this in your Value Vision Map so it guides future decisions and tradeoffs. Go to your VVM now and rank the above options in order. Then, write down the most important outcome on the line provided (I'm including a visual below as well).

Remember, there can only be one most important outcome! This does not mean that if you pick legacy, you will get no money. No! It means that in the face of a choice (or negotiation) during your exit, you will make the decision that best supports your most important outcome.

Most Important Outcome Exercise

Rank the following in order of importance, from most to least.

____ Money: Value

____ Money: Cash

____ Legacy

____ My People

____ A Place for Me

____ Sailing Off Into the Sunset

My Most Important Outcome Is: _____

_____

Your Exit Timeline – Start with the End in Mind

An exit doesn't happen overnight. It's earned and takes time, and the more time you give yourself, the better the outcome. We're talking more cash, less stress, and fewer surprises in due diligence.

One notable commonality I see with all of the companies we have worked with is that most entrepreneurs exit sooner than they plan. In the most extreme case, I assisted the owner of a chiropractic practice in developing a ten-year exit strategy. But six months later, she was selling her business.

Is this because you are a poor predictor of the future? Well, yes. Life is unpredictable. Humans are uncontrollable. And the most unpredictable and uncontrollable humans I know? Entrepreneurs (takes one to know one). Unbeknownst to our employees, our customers, and the general public, entrepreneurs aren't some mythical creatures. We are real people, with real people problems and real people opportunities. In my experience, 95% of us will exit our businesses for reasons we cannot predict, including burnout, other opportunities, changes in our spouse or family, illness, and even death. What was the reason my chiropractic client moved up her timeline significantly? Her mother developed stage four breast cancer, and she wanted to move back to the East Coast to spend their last months together. No business success would ever replace that time for her.

We cannot control our future. What we can control is choosing to run our company every day, like we can exit, which ultimately means profitably and efficiently. (Who doesn't want that?) And let's be honest, why are we doing all of this work to maximize value for someone else to enjoy? Get the value **now** for yourself and enjoy it for a few years, then pass it on!

Run your company every day like you are preparing for an exit, and you will run a better business.

The second most frequently asked question I get (we'll cover number one later) is, "When should I start my exit strategy?" You should start running your business like you are in the Exit Phase from day one: profitable, efficient, and valuable. So, if one of the unforeseen events I mentioned were to occur, you would be ready to go. The industry line is that the first day you start your business should be the first day you start your exit strategy. Come on, no one does that. When you enter any new business, you focus on the short-term immediate needs of the company, not its exit plan. (Shh! I didn't tell you this, but most exit "experts" haven't even started **their** exit plan.)

So, my direct advice is that if you haven't started your exit strategy and are reading this book, you should start today. If you picked up this book (or someone is forcing you to read it), you are already heading down the exit path, whether you know it or not.

Still, you probably think (just like everyone does when they ask the question), Jess, can you just give me a *sample timeline*? And the answer is yes, I can. Just know that I have already warned you not to put this off anymore!

The Reverse Timeline Exercise

A reverse timeline is not a new concept; it involves starting with the end date and goal, and then working backward to the actions required to achieve the goal. We will do that, but with your exit in mind. Grab your Value Vision Map (VVM) and go to Step 3: The Reverse Timeline. I'll also walk you through it step by step below.

Part 1: Exit (Pick a Day)

What month, day, year, and time do you want to complete your exit? Fill out that date on Part 1 of your timeline, which looks like this:

The day that you are walking out the door:

_____ / _____ / _____ at ____ :____ AM / PM

Part 2: Exit Execution (1-2 Years)

Exit Execution is the act of completing the exit. This involves selling the business, facilitating the family transition, completing the deal with employees, hiring a CEO, or other related tasks. You will need one to two years from your exit date to complete this phase. Take your exit date and give yourself at least one year to make this happen. Enter that date on Part 2 of your Reverse Timeline, which looks like this:

Begin Exit Execution on:

_____ / _____ / _____

Note: What if this day is close to today, or has even passed? If that is the case, you have two options. Stop the value improvement process and move straight to exit (skip to Chapter 8 for this), or extend your exit date.

Part 3: Prove the Model (3-5 Years)

Lenders and new owners want to see consistency. The valuation of a company is not ever based on one strong year; it is the weighted average of the last three to five years. Your goal in this timeframe is to demonstrate that the business has reliable results and upward momentum, without you having to pull all the levers. Take your exit execution date and backtrack at least three years to make this happen.

Enter that date on Part 3 of your Reverse Timeline, which looks like this:

Begin Proving the Model on:

_____ / _____ / _____

Again, this day may have already passed for you. If that is the case, you still have two options. You can extend your exit date further out. Or you can do this more quickly, knowing that some of your older, less profitable years will be in the mix. You can still move the valuation of your company, but you won't maximize it.

Part 4: Get Your House in Order (1-2 Years)

This is your runway. Your goal in this phase is to rectify any issues and establish a solid foundation of good business fundamentals. This is the core work we are doing with Exit Factor and the VORTEx Model. You should ideally give yourself one to two years to execute this process. Take your "prove the model" date and back it up at least one year to make this happen. Enter that date on Part 4 of your Reverse Timeline, which looks like this:

Begin Getting the House in Order on:

_____ / _____ / _____

Just like the previous parts, this date may have already passed you by. And again, you have two options (you always have options with me): (1) You can extend your exit date further out, or (2) you can do this more quickly, just like the step above. In the second case, you could skip the "prove the model" section altogether and focus on getting your house for the full one to two years. You may not be able to maximize your full valuation. However, it will still significantly improve your chances of being able to exit your business as the Elite 13% we discussed earlier in Chapter One.

Now, you have your timeline and plan. However, there is a significant difference between **planning** and **preparing.** It's not about building to sell or building to exit; it's about building to be ready for an exit at any given time. That way, when the opportunity comes (or when life throws you a curveball), you're not scrambling.

THE Springsteen Story: A Lesson in Preparation

Speaking of being ready to act anytime…let me tell you the most embarrassing story of my life (yes, I'm going there).

If you know me, you know there are three men in my life: my husband, my son, and Bruce Springsteen. It is a full-blown lifestyle for my sisters and me—we've seen him over fifty times, in countless cities and three countries.

But one thing had always eluded me: meeting him.

I planned for it. I manifested it. I journaled about it. I even ended every weekly meeting of one of my networking groups by answering the question, "Who do you most want to meet?" with "Bruce Springsteen," **for three years straight.**

So, when Bruce announced a one-off stop in Denver for his book tour, thanks to a brilliant YouTube plea by local bookstore owners Len Vlahos and Kristen Gilligan (I owe you for this), I knew this was it—my moment had come.

I made my sister get up at 2 a.m. on a freezing November morning to get in line at Tattered Cover. And while we were ready to battle for position, Denverites aren't quite as intense as Jersey superfans, we were in the first five groups.

We waited seven hours in line. One hour before Bruce arrived, my sister turned to me and said, "So…what are you going to say to him?"

Panic.

I had planned for this moment my whole life, but I hadn't **prepared** for it. No script. No clever line.

I scrambled to come up with something. I decided on, "Bruce, some of the best nights of my life have been at your shows, thank you."

I rehearsed it for sixty whole minutes.

Then it was go time.

We wore custom "Jersey Girl" shirts so Bruce would know where we were from. He looked up as we walked in and said, "Jersey girls! Where are you from?"

And that's when things unraveled. I had planned to execute my line, but I didn't prepare for a conversation. I sputtered out some town, **that I'm not even from.** Then, as he leaned in for a group hug, I elbowed my sister **in the face.**

We took our photo, and as we turned to leave, **I said,** "Wait, Bruce, I forgot my line."

He paused. "Okay?"

I turned to him, face-to-face, and said, "Some of the best nights of my life have been at your shows."

He looked at me, if I'm honest, a little nervous, and said, "Okay, honey." And then his PR woman rushed me off the stage.

The Point?

I spent my whole life **planning** for that moment, but when it came, I hadn't **prepared** for it.

Your business is no different. You can visualize, hope, and manifest a great outcome. But if you're not ready when the moment arrives and you haven't prepared for it? You'll elbow your sister in the face (metaphorically, of course).

That's why this chapter and program are about building readiness and dreaming big. So when your Springsteen moment arrives, you don't just survive it...you nail it.

(And Bruce, if you're somehow reading this, I swear I'm well prepared for our next conversation.)

Your Exit Option—Choose Plan A and a Backup

Let's clear the air: Everyone in my industry will tell you that you need an exit plan, but I'm here to tell you that you don't need a plan, you need options. Who has ever designed a plan and executed it perfectly? Because if there's one universal truth in business, it's this: **plans change.**

Here are the five core exit options again:

1. **Organized Dissolution** – Sometimes, walking away *strategically* can put more cash in your pocket than a sale.
2. **Transition to Family** – Statistically, it's rare for a business to make it to the third generation, but when done well? That's legacy.
3. **Sell to Employees** – ESOPs and internal deals can be effective, but the key is to identify the next great leader.
4. **Sell to a Third Party** – The most common route, which can include selling to an individual, a competitor, an

investment firm such as a private equity firm, or even going public.
5. **Hire a CEO** – You keep ownership, but someone else runs the show. It's more than a hire; it's a handoff. Think investor, not operator.

Each option requires different structures, financials, and expectations, so this phase is foundational. I'm not asking you to commit to one option now fully. We'll review these in more detail in Phase 5, along with the buyer types that accompany them.

However, you should try to identify your primary target option and a backup that you can execute should the worst happen. Go to your Value Vision Map, include it, and update it annually, along with any necessary actions to achieve that option.

Establish Your Exit Option

My Primary Exit Option is: _____

_____

My Backup Exit Option is: _____

_____

Your Finances—Match the Money to the Vision

How much money do you need to support the next stage of your life? To support your inspiring vision? Do you know? And do you have enough saved to accomplish that should this exit not come to fruition or not reach the level you expect?

The Exit Factor

This book is not about personal wealth, but I have strong opinions about entrepreneurs and their finances, mainly because I lived it myself. That first business I sold? The money was all gone within two years. And it was not a small amount of money. The scarier part is that I have seen hundreds of business owners end up in similar situations or worse, being unable to exit their business for any amount of money and having no personal capital saved up.

The Exit Planning Institute estimates that 80-90% of an entrepreneur's wealth is tied up in the business that they own. And many of them make the mistake of overrelying on the outcome of their exit to fund their personal wealth.

One of the worst situations I have ever encountered in my career was with an older woman, Susan, who owned an ice cream shop. She had bought the shop with her corporate retirement funds…all of them. She then spent the next fifteen years building and growing the store as a mecca in her small town. People loved to come to it. Not only did she have the best ice cream in the city, but she also had a classic candy shop where parents could reminisce and purchase their favorite childhood candies. She even had those mechanical cars and animals that kids loved to play on out in front of the store while dripping ice cream all over. The place was quintessential for a small town, and Susan took pride in it. She built exactly the business she had dreamed of.

One problem: because of her focus on the customer experience rather than the financials, the store had never generated much of a profit beyond her modest $30,000 annual owner's salary. Now, she was seventy-two and facing a debilitating health issue. She didn't have good health insurance, no disability insurance, and no savings to speak of, and she could no longer work. She needed to sell the store, and she needed to do it immediately. Unfortunately, it sold for only $55,000, about 1.8 years of her annual earnings. With no savings and her money scheduled to run out quickly, she had to move in with her son and have him support her, an act that broke her heart.

I don't tell you this story to make you feel bad for Susan or condemn her for how she ran her business. I tell you this story for you. Most of you are not in Susan's extreme situation, but you are in a situation where your finances do not support your plans. Fortunately, we plan to take care of that; it is the last piece of your Value Vision Map, where you determine how much your future will cost.

Step 1: What Will It Cost?

The goal is to enter a dollar amount you will need in assets to support your future lifestyle or next phase of life. To complete this, you should develop a personal financial plan. Whether you have an existing plan or not, please meet with your financial advisor to review, complete, or update your plan. It will be helpful to also provide your financial advisor with your expected exit value (step 2) to have an entirely accurate picture.

My Wealth Goal is: _____

_____

Step 2: What's Your Business Worth?

To know your entire wealth picture, you need to understand what your business is worth and the exit goal price for the future. Understanding your business value is not just an essential exercise for exit, but a good metric and key performance indicator (KPI) to track related to your business at all times. Determining the accurate value of your business requires expertise, and it's not an exercise you should leave to a free business calculator online or an estimate from your financial advisor. On the next page, I'll provide you with full details on obtaining an accurate estimate of your business value and how it is calculated.

My Business Value is: _____

_____

My Business Value Goal is: _____

_____

Step 3: What's the Gap?

Now that you know your goal and value, you need to do some math. Take your current assets and add your current business value. The result is your current wealth number. Now subtract that from your wealth goal. That result is called your wealth gap. Finally, subtract your current business value from your business value goal. What you have calculated is called your value gap. This number tells you what you need to make up.

Wealth Goal - Current Wealth = _____ (Wealth Gap)

Business Value Goal - Current Value = _____ (Value Gap)

Valuation Essentials

I extensively delve into business valuation in my first book, *Getting the Most for Selling Your Business*, but here is a quick recap for those who haven't read it or don't have a complete understanding.

Phase 1: Value

Business valuation isn't magic; it's a bit of art and science. Here are the basics.

Buyers pay for performance: the numbers, systems, and track record your business already has in place.

There are three standard valuation approaches:

1. **Asset-Based**: What you own (assets) minus what you owe (liabilities).
2. **Income-Based**: What your business is projected to earn in the future, adjusted to today's dollars.
3. **Market-Based**: What similar businesses sold for (this is the gold standard in determining value if you want a financial exit in the future).

The Valuation Formula That Matters

The market method has a simple formula: EBITDA x Multiple = Value.

EBITDA, earnings before interest, taxes, depreciation, and amortization, is a calculation of your earnings on a business. You don't need to become a valuation expert. You or your accountant can easily calculate this number using your Profit and Loss statement. Typically, we will examine a weighted average of the last three to five years. You can't base a company's value alone on one great year. There must be a proven history of consistent and predictable performance in terms of a company's profitability.

EBITDA—The Metric That Darth Vader Built

For all my fellow business nerds, have you ever wondered where EBITDA came from? I mean, this fancy-sounding acronym pops up in every valuation conversation, investor pitch, and broker meeting like it's been around since the dawn of capitalism.

But nope. It started with one guy: John Malone.

If that name rings a bell, it should. Malone is a media mogul and billionaire real estate tycoon. He's been called the "Cable Cowboy," but on Wall Street, his nickname was straight out of Star Wars: **Darth Vader**. That's how intense and strategic he was when building his empire.

In the 1970s, Malone was running TCI (Tele-Communications Inc.), a scrappy cable company based in Colorado that would dominate the industry. But he ran into a problem: the usual financial metrics, like net income and earnings per share, didn't make sense for fast-growing, capital-heavy companies like his.

So, he did what entrepreneurs do best: he got creative. He stripped out all non-cash expenses (such as depreciation and amortization), ignored financing decisions (including interest), and excluded the tax impact. What he was left with was a cleaner, sharper number that answered one critical question:

How much raw cash is this business generating from operations?

That's how **EBITDA** was born.

Malone used it to evaluate the actual earning power of high-growth businesses. The investing world followed suit. Private equity firms, brokers, and buyers began looking at companies in the same way, and they still do today.

Here's why this matters for you, even if you're not building the next media empire:

EBITDA is one of the most important KPIs to track as a business owner. It tells you if your business produces a return on time, energy, and money. Not someday. Not "if everything goes according to plan." Right now.

Think of it as your ROI checkpoint, because if you're not getting a strong return, why are you still doing this?

Add-Backs Are Out. And No, You Can't Expense Your Cabo Trip.

When I started in mergers and acquisitions (M&A), no business owners knew what an "add-back" was. You could mention EBITDA at a networking event and get blank stares. Fast-forward a couple of decades, and everyone's a valuation expert, armed with spreadsheets and a long list of "adjustments" to boost their bottom line.

And let me tell you, some of those lists are *creative*.

I once reviewed the financials of a construction company that included lease payments for *fourteen* Lamborghinis. I'm not sure how much drywall you can haul in a Lambo, but apparently, they were ready to find out. I've also seen business expenses for world cruises, personal divorce settlements, and even grooming for the office dog, twice a week.

Here's the reality check: **that era is over**, buyers, and more so the bankers who fund them, are tired of the smoke and mirrors. Lenders want clean books, not a scavenger hunt for the real numbers.

That's why in this program, we stick to the **core EBITDA adjustments**:

- Interest
- Taxes
- Depreciation
- Amortization

That's it. No fluff, no fiction.

Yes, we'll help you clean up your financials. That's what Phase 2: Optimize is all about. But it won't be by padding earnings with every questionable expense from the past five years. We're playing a smarter game. A cleaner business brings stronger offers, better financing, and less drama in due diligence.

> ***There are hundreds of more innovative ways to reduce your taxable income than running unnecessary expenses through your business.***

The Magic Multiplier and How to Get a Higher One

The multiple is where your exit strategy comes in. It reflects risk, industry norms, business size, team structure, and dozens of other factors we will tackle in this program.

The stronger your business, the higher your multiple will be.

There is a *large* range of multiples for every industry. For example, as of the publication of this book, businesses generating between $1 and $25 million in revenue in the healthcare industry receive a multiple of EBITDA ranging from 1x to 18.2x (excluding outliers). But what makes a company worth the lower end of that range versus the higher? That is where the qualitative factors, all the intangible assets you have built in your business, come into play.

At Exit Factor, we've identified seventy-five different qualitative factors that drive your multiple higher or lower (each conveniently broken out into our five distinct phases of the VORTEx Model). The good news? You don't need a perfect score on all seventy-five factors. In the thousands of companies we've worked with, we've found that focusing on improving three to five factors per year drives the business forward.

We will address these factors in each phase of the VORTEx Model as you complete your exercises, but in general, the categories are:

- Profitability – Clean margins and consistent earnings.
- People – A team that can operate without constant direction.
- Processes – Documented systems that reduce owner dependence.

- Customers – Strong retention, recurring revenue, and diversified base.
- Growth trajectory – A clear path for future performance without significant capital investment.

These are the levers that increase your multiple and your options. Just know this: **your value isn't fixed, it's developed over time.**

Exit Assessments, Business Valuations, or Business Appraisals?

I'm sure you have wondered many times (even late at night) what your business is worth and how it compares to your peers. There are three different methods of collecting information about your company and its performance.

1. Business Valuation: Understanding Your Company's Economic Value

A business valuation determines the overall economic value of your company at a *specific point in time*. This process is crucial to understanding your company's worth *today*, whether for sale, merger, or other financial decisions.

2. Business Appraisal: A Snapshot of Specific Assets

A business appraisal is a detailed evaluation of specific assets at a particular time. This process is often used for insurance, loans, or taxes. It focuses on estimating the value of tangible and intangible assets such as real estate, machinery, or intellectual property.

3. Exit Assessment: The Strategic Tool for Business Growth

Unique to Exit Factor, the Exit Assessment is designed specifically for businesses planning for their future. This assessment establishes your business's current value, similar to a traditional valuation, and provides actionable insights into what needs to change, both financially and operationally, to achieve your goals. The Exit Assessment evaluates your financial performance, market position, and growth potential, offering key performance indicators (KPIs) and objectives to maximize your business's value and profitability. Connecting with one of our certified Exit Factor consultants to guide you through the process may be helpful. A complete overview of the Exit Assessment is included in the toolkit provided at exitfactorbook.com.

However you assess the valuation and performance of your business, you need to gain a comprehensive understanding and comparison with industry peers to identify where your company stands in relation to theirs. There may be profitability issues that need to be addressed, such as gross and net margins that

> fall out of line with industry standards for companies of your size, as well as operational issues that impact the quality of your company. The results will allow you to identify benchmarks, KPIs, and a minimum profitability bar for your company (more on this in Phase 2: Optimize).

Here's Where It All Comes Together: Your Value Vision Map

We are almost done with the basics you need to know to prepare to exit your company. We've walked the Value Vision Map together. Now it's time to take action. This is where strategy meets reality, and you begin to lead your exit, rather than waiting for one to happen to you.

The VVM is your roadmap for what comes next. Fill it out now, and revisit it as you move through each phase of the program. Because the more you can see your exit, the more confidently you'll build your path to it.

Case Study: Chris's Value Vision Map

Remember Chris? I bet you thought I forgot about him. And if you didn't read the introduction, you'd better go back and do that now, it's essential for the rest of our journey. When Chris and I completed his Value Vision Map, here's what we came up with.

Inspiring Future:
Chris wanted out of the business and wanted to spend time raising his kids. They were in second and fifth grade when we started working together, and he was acutely aware that he had only a few "golden" years left before they no longer thought hanging out with Dad was cool. He planned not to work again until his youngest child was in high school, and then Chris would search for another business to buy or re-enter the corporate world.

Identify Your Top Exit Priorities:
Money – Cash. Chris hadn't saved a lot over the last few years. He had plowed most of his savings back into the business. So, money to afford time at home with the family was paramount.

Establish Timeline:
This exercise was challenging for Chris because he wanted to leave immediately, but based on his goals and the state of the business, he knew that wasn't possible. Here was the plan we came up with:

- 1/2/2025 at 5:00 p.m.: Exit Date
- 1/2/2024: Start his exit execution
- 2022 and 2023: Get his house in order

You'll notice we decided to skip "prove the model." Chris knew he would be leaving money on the table because a potential lender would be averaging his 2021 (and maybe his 2020) numbers into his final valuation, which were not good. However, he decided that the risk and the value left would be worth it to reach his goal faster.

Ideal Exit Option:
Chris decided a sale was best, with the backup being to sell to a group of key employees. He knew his employees didn't have a lot of money and would be hesitant to borrow from a bank, which would mean he would have to provide seller financing.

Finances That Support the Vision:
Chris had an Exit Assessment done, and he hired a new financial planner to update his personal financial plan with accurate goals and values based on his new vision for the future.

Wealth Goal: $7 million
Current Wealth: $2.5 million
Wealth Gap: $4.5 million
Value Goal: $5 million
Current Value: $2 million
Value Gap: $3 million

You will notice that Chris's wealth gap exceeded his value gap, meaning that improving business value alone would not get Chris to his goals. This situation is very common. But it's a simple solution. Along the journey of improving his business value, Chris increased his earnings. He used that money to invest in other assets, thereby increasing his wealth beyond the value of the business.

I learned this crucial fact from a brilliant client: the most successful entrepreneurs typically generate the majority of their wealth outside of their businesses. They operate a highly profitable business and then use those profits to reinvest in other areas, improving their wealth portfolio so they are **not solely dependent on an exit to achieve their wealth goals**.

> ### Your Move
>
> **Reflection**
>
> You have to know where you are going before you can carve a path. Even if you have thought about your goals before, complete the Value Vision Map in its entirety.
>
> **Simple Action Step**
>
> *Complete, or revisit, your Value Vision Map.*
>
> Make sure you've defined your exit goal, your wealth number, your timeline, and your preferred exit paths. If you've already filled it out, review it. Does it still reflect your vision?
>
> **Tool to Use**
>
> Download the **Value Vision Map Worksheet** at exitfactorbook.com. This guided template helps you define your future, select your priorities, and create a reverse-engineered plan that leads to a meaningful exit.

Chapter 5

PHASE 2: OPTIMIZE YOUR FINANCIALS

Increase Profit to Drive Value

Where We Are in the VORTEx

Welcome to Phase 2 of the Exit Factor program: **Optimize.** Now, we start unlocking hidden value inside your business.

VORTEx MODEL

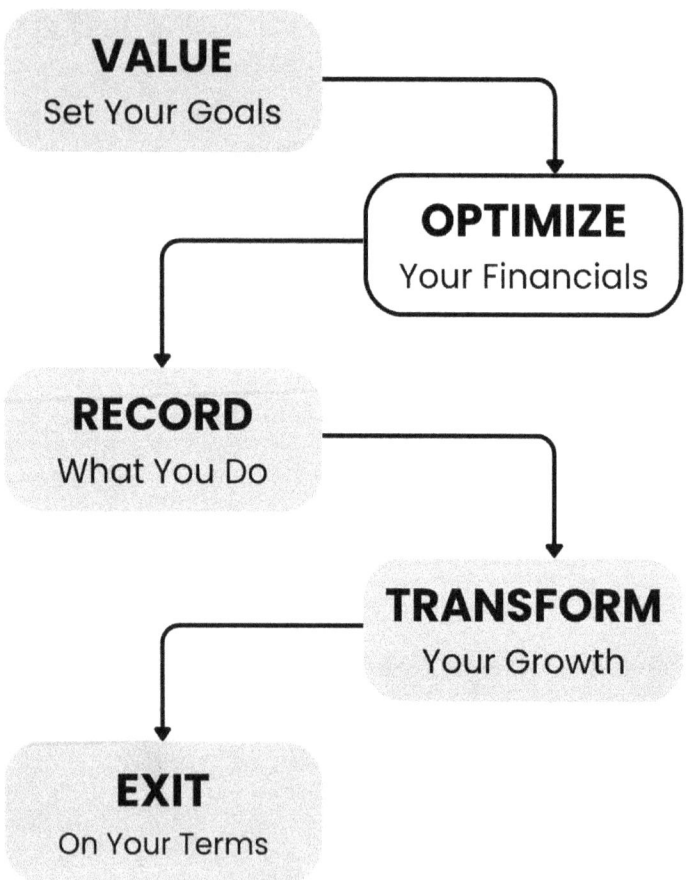

Until now, we've focused on defining the value you want to create and understanding what your business is currently worth. Now, we shift our focus to making your business more profitable.

Let's be clear: profit is power. It gives you options, fuels growth, and drives your exit value. And while chasing revenue can feel exciting, profit delivers a higher multiple at exit.

In this chapter, you'll learn how to analyze your numbers through a tool we call the **Profit Pulse Plan** and start thinking like a financial steward, not just a founder.

What We'll Cover in This Phase:
- The basics of understanding profit
- How to clean up and interpret financial statements
- Implementing the Profit Pulse Plan to drive profit and value in your business

Many business owners find these topics boring, but trust me, it's all about perspective.

Once you learn to manage the numbers, you can write your next chapter with more cash in your pocket and much less chaos in your business.

What Is Profit, Really?

Before we can optimize profit, we need to define what it is. Because here's the thing: most business owners throw the word "profit" around without clarity. And before you think this is too basic or beneath you, I want to remind you that sometimes, when we get too deeply entrenched in our business or become too large, we forget how to do the basics well. Many business owners throw around statements like, "We made a profit last year." Great. But what kind?

I was working with a client who was distraught because they had just been to an industry conference where a group of their competitors were quoting 65% profit margins. When my clients asked, 'Is that gross profit or net?' They said net profit. My clients were not making close to that; they were at 15% at best.

When we reviewed their industry metrics, we found that they were not only in line with but also above the net profit in their industry. At the next industry meetup, my client pushed his colleague further and asked, "So, with your 65% net margin, you guys must be rolling in cash, huh?"

And the competitor replied, "Oh no! I haven't taken a distribution in years. Actually, we just had to take on some debt to save the business."

He discovered that his competitor was unaware that gross margin is not the same as net profit; he was quoting him the wrong number. My client kindly provided him with the quick overview I'm about to give you, and his colleague graciously thanked him. The moral of the story? This conversation took place between two sophisticated technology founders who each generated seven to eight-figure revenue figures. No matter how fluent you are in a business's financial aspects, a review of the basics never hurts.

Financials Are the Language of Leadership

Most of us didn't start our businesses to become accountants, but we *did* sign up to be responsible for the financial future of something we built. Owning the numbers isn't optional. It's leadership.

Financials are the language we all need to be fluent in. Restated in another way, probably by the best business owner of all time, Warren Buffett states, "Accounting is the language of business."

Buffett also credits his mentor, Benjamin Graham, his professor of accounting at Columbia Business School, for this mindset. In Buffett's words, accounting gave him the language to evaluate businesses. He even once joked that Graham said, "If you're not willing to learn the language of accounting, you really shouldn't be picking stocks yourself." I'm going to reframe that for our conversation:

> ***If you are not willing to learn and master the language of financials, you shouldn't be running a business.***

Our primary responsibility as business owners is to be good financial stewards of the company. If the company doesn't make a profit this year and we have to take on debt, it's our fault. If the company runs out of money and fails, it's our fault. Not the CFO, not the accountant: only the company's owners, CEO, and founders have the full weight and responsibility for the financial integrity of our companies.

With that said, let's make sure we have these basics correct.

The Three Types of Profit That Matter

There are three different types of profit in your business, and they are not interchangeable:

- **Gross Profit** is your revenue minus direct costs (like materials and labor). It tells you if your core product or service is profitable.
- **Net Profit** is the amount left after all expenses, including overhead, interest, and taxes. This metric indicates whether your organization supports sales of your product

or service. It is also commonly referred to as your bottom line.
- **EBITDA** (Earnings Before Interest, Taxes, Depreciation, and Amortization) is the metric we use throughout Exit Factor, as it strips away non-operational and one-time variables. It's the clearest view of operational profitability and the return on investment you get from owning your business.

A unique perspective in this book is that we do not believe net income tells the whole story. I reviewed this in depth in the previous chapter, but remember that EBITDA gives the clearest view of how well your business performs.

Cash Is King (Even When You're Profitable)

One of my favorite quotes in business finance is from Verne Harnish: "Revenue is vanity, profit is sanity." His colleague Alan Miltz adds the final punch: "But cash is king."

This book doesn't have time to cover cash and cash management, so I recommend Alan and Verne's extensive coverage in their book, *Scaling Up*. If you are in a business that involves inventory, accounts receivable, work in progress, or heavy capital investment (or, honestly, any industry), you must manage your cash as effectively as your profit.

Just because your P&L shows a profit doesn't mean that money is available to spend. Profit is theoretical, cash is real. And the gap between the two is where businesses can get into real trouble.

Phase 2: Optimize Your Financials

Follow the Money, Understanding Your Financials

Your financial statements are not just for your CPA. They are the map of your business's health and your most powerful tool for identifying where profit is leaking.

There are five core financial documents every owner should understand:

DOCUMENT	WHAT IT SHOWS
Profit and Loss (P&L) Statement	Revenue, expenses, and income *over time*
Balance Sheet	Assets, liabilities, and earnings at a *snapshot in time*
Cash Flow Statement	How money moves through your business *in real-time*
Tax Return	What you've reported to the IRS *validates* your other financial documents
Bank Statements	The unfiltered truth: what's actually in the bank *to spend*

Financial Health Check: Who sends you these reports? When do you receive them—monthly, quarterly, annually? Do you receive all the reports or just the P&L? How much time do you spend reviewing them, or do you simply file them away?

117

If you're not receiving these or don't understand them, you don't have a grip on your business. And if your reports are incomplete, inconsistent, or cash-based only, your valuation (and ability to exit) takes a hit.

When you understand how profit moves through these reports, you gain control. When they conflict or don't exist, your value and options erode.

How It All Comes Together

Each document tells part of the story. But it's only when all of the papers align that you get a true story of how your business is operating.

My son once made me buy a puzzle with 100 pieces, all different shades of blue. It was supposed to form a shark. The problem? He lost the box top before we put it together. No picture, no reference, just an ocean of confusion. After fifteen minutes, he got frustrated: "Why can't *you* just put it together?"

That's precisely how most business owners feel when they look at their numbers. You have five different financial documents, each with many line items and totals that feel related, but no clear view of how the pieces connect. And when it comes time to exit your business, that confusion can cost you, literally.

When you go to sell your business, your buyer (or their banker) will compare **all five** of these documents.

If those numbers don't line up? They won't assume you made a mistake; they'll assume that you don't know how your business runs. Or worse, you're hiding something. That's enough to tank a deal, slash your valuation, or spook lenders.

This situation is why optimizing your profit isn't just about getting your P&L to show a positive number. It's about **telling one consistent financial story** across every document. Let's break that down.

How Profit Flows Through Your Business

Once your net profit is calculated on your **P&L**, it doesn't just sit there.

Step 1: Profit Earned—Profit & Loss Statement (P&L)

Your business earns revenue and pays expenses. What's left over is your net profit. This number shows the health of your operations, how effectively your business generates value through its day-to-day activities. It's the first point that proves your model works.

Step 2: Profit Recorded—Balance Sheet and Tax Return

That net profit doesn't disappear. It is reflected in your retained earnings on your balance sheet and is reported on your annual tax return. This step demonstrates your company's long-term financial health. It's how a lender or buyer confirms that your profitability is real and consistent. It's also where your financial hygiene, or lack of it, becomes very visible.

Step 3: Profit Realized—Cash Flow Statement and Bank Accounts

Now comes the most critical (and often most misunderstood) part: just because profit is reported doesn't mean it shows up in your bank account. Your cash flow statement tracks whether the business is generating usable, accessible cash or if inventory, debt payments, or poor cash controls are eating up that profit. This step is where investors and buyers assess whether your earnings are genuine or merely theoretical.

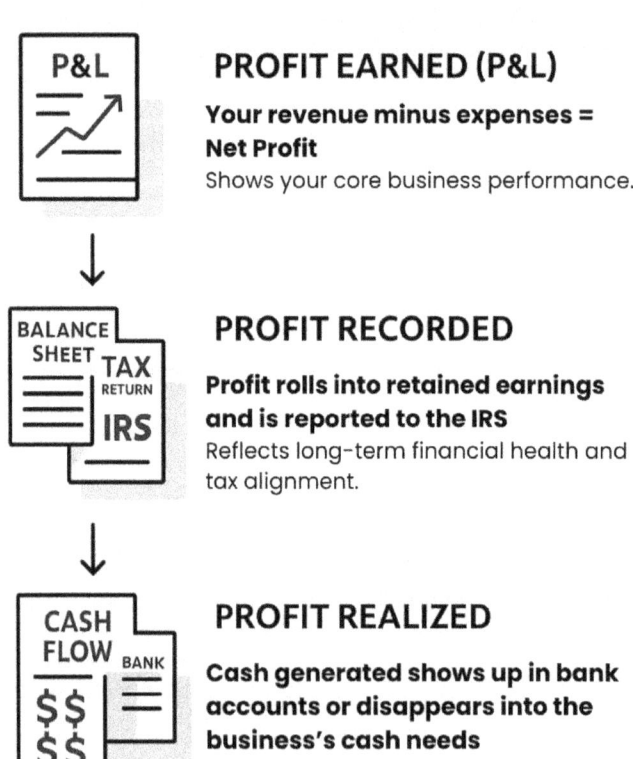

The One Number Buyers Care About: EBITDA

When your financials are **aligned across all documents**, you tell a trustworthy story:

- Your P&L shows substantial profit.
- Your Balance Sheet shows healthy retained earnings.
- Your Cash Flow Statement shows financial stability.
- Your Bank Statements confirm that there is real money in the bank.
- Your Tax Return backs it up legally.

That's the kind of business investors, buyers, and bankers can trust, and one they assign a premium valuation to.

Now that you understand where the numbers live and how they connect, let's focus on the one that matters most to your business's value and future freedom: EBITDA.

Profit Over Revenue

Let's shatter a common myth: you don't need to grow to become profitable. If your current model isn't working, more revenue makes the leak bigger. It's like pouring water into a bucket with holes; the faster you pour it in, the faster it falls out.

That's why we start with profit. Fixing your margins gives you breathing room:

- More cash for yourself
- More budget for improvements
- More clarity on whether your model works

From this point forward, you'll use **EBITDA** as your primary profit metric.

So going forward, you'll track two things:

- Your EBITDA (dollar amount)
- Your EBITDA Margin (as a percentage of revenue)

Ask yourself: Would you be satisfied if your business stayed at its current profit percentage for the next five years?

Now, the exercise I am about to introduce to you is simple. Sometimes too simple. Typically, when we teach this topic to owners, they tell us they have already done the work, shaved all expenses, and cannot see how they can improve anymore. I promise you, this process uncovers hidden profit *every single time*. So stay with me.

Introducing The Profit Pulse Plan

The **Profit Pulse Plan** is a straightforward quarterly exercise that helps you identify hidden expenses, enhance margins, and operate a leaner, more profitable business. It's the only tool we use with every single Exit Factor client.

The truth is that every one of us has **expense creep** in our business.

It's like mold…quiet, sneaky, and spreading in places you're not looking.

If you've ever paid for something you're not using anymore, congratulations, you're human. I'm guilty too.

There's the yoga studio I haven't set foot in for six months…but they keep charging my card, and I keep thinking, *Next month, I'll go.*

There's that app I signed up for during a free trial and forgot to cancel. (Thanks, Apple.)

And yes, my Showtime subscription lives on, long after *Billions* wrapped and my reason for having the channel disappeared.

Now multiply that by ten, and that's what's probably happening in your business.

The bigger your team, the more hands touching spending decisions, the more invisible waste builds up. Forgotten software tools, overstuffed marketing retainers, overlapping services, "temporary" contractors you forgot to turn off. It's all in there.

**This is why the Profit Pulse Plan works—
it surfaces all those "forgotten" dollars so you can
stop paying for ghosts.**

And no judgment. We all do it. But when you clean it up, you'll be shocked at how much profit you can reclaim without cutting anything that matters.

Exit Factor Toolkit: Don't forget you can download the entire toolkit for this book at exitfactorbook.com or just walk through the sections below.

The 4-Step Profit Pulse Plan (PPP)

Step 1: Where Are You Now?

Grab your last twelve months of P&L data and fill in the summary metrics below on your PPP. Or if you want, you can jot them down below:

- Total Revenue: _____
- Total Expenses: _____
- EBITDA: _____
- EBITDA Margin% (EBITDA ÷ Revenue): _____%

Looking at these numbers in black and white, I want you to reflect: Is this profit, this return, worth the investment of your hours, risk, and stress that you put into your business?

Step 2: Cut the Clutter

Once you have completed step 1, you are ready to move on. Return to your bookkeeping system and generate a detailed profit and loss statement for the past twelve months. It should show every expense, vendor, and transaction. Yes, I know it's a long report.

It might feel like a mess at first. That's okay. This process isn't about judgment. It's about seeing what's going on.

Start by auditing your top three expense categories, but eventually, I want you to go through them all. It's also easiest to start with Operating Expenses versus Cost of Goods. Often, we have more waste in the former.

Now, go line by line. And for every single expense listed in the report, I want you to ask yourself two questions:

Phase 2: Optimize Your Financials

1. **Is this necessary for my business to operate?**

    The key here is necessary, not "nice to have," not "maybe next quarter," not "we may need this thing if x,y, or z potentially happens in the future." We are talking about the **necessary.**

2. **Is this working in my business?**

    The key here: Is this working for us, producing results? If it's software, is it efficient and reliable? If it's hardware or equipment, is it functioning correctly and in good working order, or does it cost more to maintain than it's worth? If it's a marketing campaign, is it producing closed, profitable deals?

If the answer is no to either question, record that expense on the sheet provided in your Profit Pulse Plan (PPP) in step 2. Now repeat that for every single expense. I know it's a lot of work, but it's worth it.

Finally, you need to decide what to do with the waste. This last step is the most challenging, and it's where some owners may need more help or accountability. When you look at someone else's P&L, the waste is obvious. But when is it yours? Suddenly, every expense has a story and a soulmate. The clearest insights come from outside eyes, people who aren't emotionally attached to your expenses.

So, what is the last step? Get rid of every expense you said no to. Return to your PPP, and fill in the action you will take on each wasted expense. Are you going to Eliminate it, Fix It, or Replace It?

Here is an example of a simple, working and necessary sheet that has been completed:

EXPENSE	ANNUAL COST	NECESSARY?	WORKING?	ACTION: ELIMINATE, FIX, REPLACE
Ad Agency Retainer	$36,000	N	N	Eliminate
General Liability Insurance	$18,000	Y	N	Replace
Total Expenses Saved	$54,000		Total Margin Increase	1.5%

The UPS Driver Who Became a Millionaire

Ronald Read wasn't a CEO. He didn't invent anything. He wasn't gifted equity in a startup or handed a trust fund. But when he passed away at age ninety-two, he left an estate worth over $8 million.

He was a UPS driver, gas station attendant, and janitor who lived simply, saved consistently, and invested steadily over time. The reason he made his fortune? He *multiplied* his modest income over time through patience and compounding returns.

That's not dissimilar to the multiplier effect we are trying to achieve: every dollar working smarter, not harder.

Optimizing a single expense, raising your prices by 5%, or removing one unprofitable client may seem insignificant in your business. But those decisions, multiplied over the years, can be the difference between a 3x and 7x exit.

Step 3: Set the Bar

Now that you've cleaned up your P&L, it's time to set your new **profitability standard**, your "bar." Greg Crabtree, author of *Simple Numbers, Straight Talk, Big Profits!*, refers to this as your "profit bar." It's the minimum level of profitability you're willing to accept in your business; anything below it should trigger action.

Profit First

Another powerful take on this principle comes from Mike Michalowicz in his book *Profit First*. When I read this book, I knew Mike and I were cut from the same cloth. Borrowing a phrase from him, I hope he finds it endearing, we are profit solemates.

In *Profit First*, he flips the traditional accounting formula from "Sales – Expenses = Profit" to "Sales – Profit = Expenses." In other words, take your profit off the top *first* and force your business to run with what's left. It's a simple shift that can create massive discipline. If you have not read the book, I highly recommend it.

In every business and industry, there are different levels of profitability. At Exit Factor, we help clients define their profitability targets using detailed analysis in their Exit Assessments. While we won't go that deep here, you can still use the general benchmarks below to guide your target setting.

Guidelines for Your Profit Bar:

- Below 5%: Danger Zone. You're working too hard for too little.
- 10–15%: Healthy. A solid business with room to grow.
- 20%+: Elite. Valuable, efficient, and exit-ready.

In your PPP, you are asked first to establish your profit bar. It is the minimum level of profit you are willing to accept in your business moving forward. Enter that percentage in step 3, which looks like this:

My EBITDA Bar is: _____ %

Next, you need to establish the profit levels that will trigger an action. Give yourself a buffer of two to three points. Below the range, you will cut expenses to get back into the margin, and above it, you know you are safe to reinvest in the business. Enter those percentages in step 3 as well, which looks like this:

Below _____ % I will **cut expenses**.
Above _____ % I can **reinvest in the business**.

A plan without accountability and action is likely to fail. So go beyond just setting goals. What are three actions you will commit to to help you keep in line with this new profitability plan? Some examples could be:

- Review my expenses quarterly.
- Only add new budget items after our quarterly financial review has been completed.
- Institute a system like Profit First.

Identify three actions that will help you and enter them into the last section of step 3.

Step 4: Build the Rhythm

The Profit Pulse Plan isn't a one-time activity. It's a **quarterly ritual**. Add time to your calendar once a quarter to:

- Review expenses
- Reconfirm your profit bar
- Course-correct in real-time

The goal is not just to find waste once, but to prevent it from creeping back in. Set these dates and add them to your calendar. Better yet, bring your team into this process so they can begin auditing their departments and find the waste. One of the key activities I do with my team every time they ask for an increased budget? I say, "Run a PPP first, and tell me you can't *find money* before we simply *spend more*."

To complete your PPP, enter your ongoing commitments in step 4, including:

- The date you will receive your financial reports each month moving forward.
- The recurring date(s) you commit to reviewing your expenses.
- Any leaders on your team that you will task with completing a PPP for their department.

Case Study: Same Revenue, More Profit

At 29, Brooke and Dana launched their businesses within months of each other. They didn't know it then, but their parallel paths would become a case study of two very different philosophies and outcomes.

Both were in high-touch professional services. Both were smart, passionate, and committed to building something meaningful. But their approaches? Worlds apart.

Dana came from a luxury brand background and was determined to deliver a best-in-class client experience. From day one, she invested in it all: prime office space in a downtown high-rise, custom furniture, polished brand visuals, and a marketing team that made her look like the industry's next breakout star. Every dollar that came in went back out toward upgrades, image, and expansion.

And from the outside, it worked. Dana looked wildly successful. She became the person other entrepreneurs admired: confident, stylish, and seemingly unstoppable.

Brooke, on the other hand, had no cushion. She bootstrapped from day one, and profitability wasn't optional. She didn't have the luxury of chasing brand prestige or building the "perfect" team. What she did have was discipline.

Brooke set a rule from her first client payment: every dollar had to produce at least 20% profit. That profit bar became the lens through which she made every business decision: vendor selection, pricing, and hiring. Her office was functional, not flashy. Her systems were efficient, not fancy. But her financials? Strong from day one.

Over time, both businesses grew. But the growth looked very different.

Dana's revenue climbed, but so did her stress. Her P&L consistently bled red, and she relied on credit lines to cover cash gaps. Five years in, she'd built a well-known brand, but not a business that could support her. When the pressure became too much, she sold for pennies on the dollar and returned to the corporate world to rebuild her finances.

Brooke? She was just getting started.

With her consistent margins, she began investing outside the business: a rental property, a cash balance plan, and even some fun business investments with surprisingly high returns. Five years in, Brooke had built a $10 million business with a healthy 20% margin and created a seven-figure personal investment portfolio. And she still loved showing up to work.

One was built for appearance. The other was built for endurance.

One grew fast and flamed out. The other grew wisely and built wealth.

The difference? Profit and value were the priority from day one for Brooke.

That's the power of setting your profit bar and sticking to it. Because at the end of the day, a beautiful business that drains you isn't success. It's a liability in disguise.

Phase 2: Optimize Your Financials

This phase isn't about accounting. It's about empowerment, about owning your numbers, reclaiming your margins, and stepping fully into your role as the financial leader of your company.

Case Study: Chris's Profit Pulse Plan

Before we close this chapter, let's see what this looks like in the real world. Here's how our Exit Factor client Chris used the PPP to make one of the fastest turnarounds we've seen.

When I first introduced this plan to him, he was resistant. Like many of the business owners I mentioned in the chapter, he had two limiting beliefs: (1) he believed he had to grow to achieve profitability, and (2) he thought he was running his business as lean as he possibly could.

First, we identified where he was.

Step 1: Where Are You Now?—The Profit Snapshot
- Total Revenue: $5,000,000
- Total Operating Expenses: $1,250,000
- EBITDA: -$210,000
- EBITDA Margin% (EBITDA ÷ Revenue): -4.2%

Reflection: Is this return worth the investment of your hours, risk, and stress?

Chris answered this question with a resounding no! Even though he paid himself a salary of $150,000 through the company, the numbers showed he was still losing money yearly, so he had to go into debt to keep things afloat.

Step 2: Cut the Clutter—The 80/20 Expense Review

We reviewed Chris's entire P&L and identified almost $500,000 of wasted or misused expenses. Most of it was salaries for people he didn't need (something we'll get into in the next chapter). Here's a summary of just some of the expenses we found.

EXPENSE	ANNUAL COST	NECESSARY?	WORKING?	ACTION: ELIMINATE, FIX, REPLACE
Ad Agency Retainer	$65,000	Y	N	Replace
Fractional CFO	$125,000	Y	N	Replace
Extra Salaries	$225,000	N	N	Eliminate
Misc. Expenses	$81,000	N	N	Eliminate
Total Expenses Saved	$496,000		Total Margin Increase	9.92%

Step 3: Set the Bar—Establish Your Minimum Profit Standard

Chris vowed never to fall into the red again. Based on his industry's average EBITDA margins and the exit value Chris was targeting, we decided on the following profit bar:

My EBITDA Bar is: 10%

Below 8%, I will **cut expenses.**

Above 12%, I can **reinvest in the business.**

What are the top three actions that will help keep you in line?

- Conduct a PPP every quarter.
- Review my COGS to get Gross Profit back in line
- with industry averages.
- Evaluate each deal on Gross Profit, not Revenue.

Step 4: Build the Rhythm—Financial Check-In Habits

Lastly, we needed to involve Chris's team. He had a full-time controller on board whom he trusted and was going to have her help lead the process. He also needed his team leads in Sales and Operations to start analyzing their department's spend.

- Date each month I will receive my reports: 15th of every month.
- Recurring date to review all expenses: 20th of every month.

DEPARTMENT	TEAM MEMBER RESPONSIBLE
Finance	Sue
Sales	Jack
Operations	Diane

At the end of this exercise, Chris was a full believer. He went from losing more than $200,000 to profiting $286,000 in just one quarter! Was it complicated? No. Was it hard? Yes. But was it worth it? Also yes.

Your Move

Reflection

Are you leading your business with a value-first mindset, or have you been overspending your profits?

Simple Action Step

Complete your Profit Pulse Plan.

Go to your accounting software, pull a detailed Profit & Loss statement from the last year, and work through your PPP. You can use your scheduled one hour a week over the next few weeks to complete this, or extend it to one longer session to get it done faster.

Tool to Use

Download the **Profit Pulse Plan** template at exitfactorbook.com.

This tool will walk you through the five steps of the Profit Pulse system—so you can lead your financial review like an investor, not just a busy founder.

Chapter 6

PHASE 3: RECORD WHAT YOU DO

Build a Business That Runs Without You

Where We Are in the VORTEx

Up until now, we've defined what you want (Value) and cleaned up how you make money (Optimize). This chapter is where the next shift happens: from "It's all on me" to "It's built to last without me." If you stop here, you'll have a profitable but dependent business. If you keep going, you'll have a valuable, transferable asset.

In Phase 3 of the Exit Factor program, **Record**, we begin building systems that create true freedom. Because the most valuable businesses aren't just profitable, they're transferable.

VORTEx MODEL

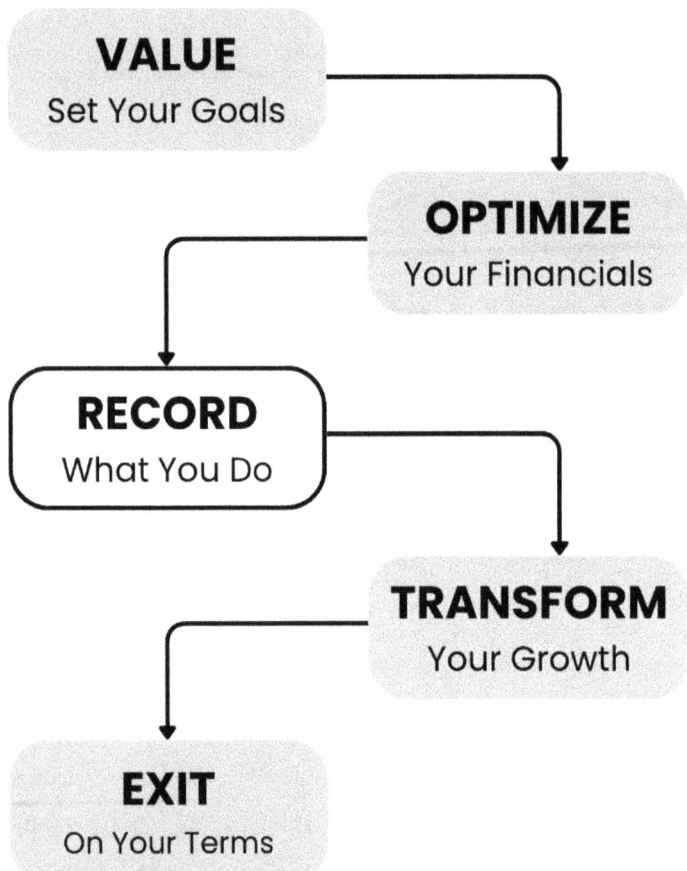

Phase 3: Record What You Do

You've probably heard the advice to "work on the business, not in the business." But what does that look like when you're still the one closing deals, solving every crisis, and approving every invoice?

I get it and have lived this life myself. In the past week, I've worn nearly every hat a business owner can wear:

- Mentoring my franchisees
- Leading sales calls and pitches
- Finalizing legal contracts
- Hosting podcast interviews
- Delivering a keynote
- Rolling out a marketing strategy
- Approving benefit plans
- Writing this book
- And yes, cleaning the conference room after a training session

All while raising a very spirited 3.5-year-old (I have no idea where he gets it from). If you're reading this nodding your head, welcome to the club. You're not alone.

Even now, as someone who teaches exit strategy for a living, I'm still working through the very systems in this book. I built Exit Factor because I needed it, first for myself, and then for my clients.

This phase is where "working on the business" becomes more than a nice idea; it becomes a trackable, step-by-step plan.

The Role Release Roadmap (3R)

If you are like most business owners, I don't have to sell you on reclaiming your time and delegating tasks and roles in your business. You get it. But how do you do it? That's the thing that always frustrates me with this topic. It's not like you go to bed one night with a jack-of-all-trades job description, think to yourself, *Tomorrow I'm going to start working on the business, not in the business*, and poof! The next morning, you are free. Wishful thinking.

This is not an overnight fix; it's a process that builds momentum every quarter. And the sooner you start, the sooner you get your life back.

The truth is that there is a strategic way to exit the roles and responsibilities in your business, and it occurs over time, sometimes spanning several years.

That's where the Role Release Roadmap (3R) comes in. This process provides a method to identify, score, and offload roles that keep your business overly dependent on you, thereby increasing the company's value over time.

It isn't just about clearing your plate: it's about removing the ***right* things, in the *right* order, so your business becomes more valuable and independent over time.**

Take one of our solar company clients who was preparing for an exit just ten months away. One advisor told him to hire a sales manager before selling. Instead, we suggested a smarter approach: employ an administrator to take on other tasks and *stay* in sales during the transition.

An investment in a high salary temporarily reduces the EBITDA of your business since the return on investment of a sales manager can take years. Yes, if he had more time, a sales manager would be a suitable option. But he didn't have years.

The result? He's now under contract with a buyer who is agreeable to the owner staying in sales for a short transition, and the deal has progressed without delay or a reduction in valuation.

The Role Release Roadmap is built around three simple, actionable components that give you a live snapshot of your workload, your risk exposure, and your most significant opportunities to let go:

- **Step 1: Get Real About Your Role** – Map out everything you do and assess the value and risk associated with each task.
- **Step 2: Score it and Sort It** – Prioritize what to offload, to whom, and when.
- **Step 3: Make the Handoff Happen** – Move through your transfer plan and complete tasks one at a time, entirely off your plate.

We'll walk through the importance of each step and how to do it, but remember, you can download all of these tools for free at exitfactorbook.com.

My goal for you is that at the end of this chapter, "working on the business" isn't just a hope in the future, but one that you can see on paper with a date assigned to it.

Why This Matters So Much (Especially to Buyers)

You won't lead your company forever. Whether your successor comes from within your team or the outside world, someone else will eventually sit in your seat.

The question is…will they have a playbook? Or will they be guessing? Because the more your business relies on you, the harder it is to scale, sell, or even step away for a few weeks.

This phase isn't about documenting processes. Many books have been written on that subject, but documentation without analysis is a waste of time. The key is to look for ways to make the entire system more efficient, especially when it comes to removing responsibilities from your plate.

You are going to walk through exactly how to:

- Identify the roles you are still holding on to.
- Score them based on value and risk to your business.
- Let go of the right responsibilities, in the right order.

By the end of this chapter, you'll have a concrete plan to reduce owner dependence, increase transferability, and free yourself up to lead like an investor, not just talk about it.

Why Owner-Reliance Kills Value

Let's talk about value and what drives it in a buyer's eyes.

You probably have heard that buyers don't love owner-dependent businesses. But, in this phase, we're going to fix that.

Think of it this way: the more people who *can* run your company, the more people who *will* want to buy it. And if more people want it, more competition is generated, and you get paid a higher price.

So, who are these buyers?

When I speak to groups of entrepreneurs, I always ask them to guess what percentage of the business buyer market falls into these categories:

- Investment buyers like private equity (PE) firms.
- Strategic and synergistic buyers, including your competitors or businesses in similar industries.
- Individual buyers.

Phase 3: Record What You Do

Almost every group gets it wrong.

- Only **10%** of buyers in the main street and lower middle market are private equity firms.
- Another **10%** are strategic or synergistic buyers.
- The remaining **80%**? They're **individual buyers**, usually first-time entrepreneurs coming out of corporate jobs.

I discuss Sara Blakely's exit journey later in this book, but one of the practices I adopted early in my career from her was dedicating a theme to each day: Mondays for sales, Tuesdays for marketing, and so on. The practice made me more efficient, however, it is not a good strategy to achieve your goal as an exited owner!

Here's the catch: if we want real competition for our companies and real value, we have to make them easier to buy.

Most buyers are specialists, not generalists.

But not in the way you think. Not a specialist in your industry, but a specialist in one functional area. Most buyers have a core competency in *one functional area*: typically sales, operations, or management. Unlike you, they are not used to wearing five hats and juggling everything from hiring to client fires to vendor negotiations. So, the more hats you wear, the harder it is to find someone willing to run your company.

Here's what that looks like in practice:

- Currently, if you want someone to take over your role who is willing to wear all the hats you do, you would have to find that one unicorn buyer. And then you're at that

145

- buyer's mercy and will have to accept whatever deal they provide you.
- Now, let's say you can eliminate just a few roles: legal, HR, and public relations. You may have ten people willing to take over. There is interest, but not competition.
- But what if you get yourself out of every role except one or two, such as management and mentoring? Suddenly, you have a pool of thousands of buyers and intense competition for your business.

More buyers mean more competition, which in turn leads to more value.

Even private equity and strategic buyers think this way. They don't want to buy your company and then scramble to replace three key roles to keep the lights on.

The less your business relies on you, the more attractive and valuable it becomes.

So let's get started with the Role Release Roadmap…

Step 1: Get Real About Your Role

Now that we understand the issue, how can we resolve it? You need to start by getting brutally honest about your role.

Most business owners think they know what they do all day… but they don't. The truth? You're in way deeper than you realize.

That's why the first step I will suggest is a little boring. And most people hate doing it, including me! However, I have found in business that the most basic, tedious tasks often yield the highest results.

Phase 3: Record What You Do

I want you to document everything you do for the next two weeks, and I mean everything. Choose two weeks that represent your typical day-to-day life as the owner. Skip the vacation week or the annual retreat. You want a real picture of your regular workload.

And don't just track 9 to 5—we all know the workday rarely fits in those lines.

You can use whatever system works for you:

- A time-tracking app,
- The 3R sheet provided, or
- My favorite option is to print your calendar and scribble the tasks you handle between meetings.

Once you've captured your full scope of responsibilities, go to the 3R sheet and plug in the estimated number of hours per week you spent on each task.

Here's an example of the past week I just described for myself above.

ROLE/TASK	DESCRIPTION	HOURS PER WEEK
Franchisee Coaching	Met with three franchisees	1.5
Management Meeting	Sales Meeting	0.5
Sales Calls	Two prospect calls + follow-up	3
Legal Review	New vendor negotiation	2
Client Session	ABC Construction quarterly	2

ROLE/TASK	DESCRIPTION	HOURS PER WEEK
Podcast Guesting	Interview for franchise publication	1.5
Marketing Strategy Review	Reviewed with the new CMO	1.5
Benefits Review	Set up for Prospere Team	1
Updated Training Materials	Prep for training week	3

This exercise gives you a clear snapshot of what you're doing and what's clogging up your capacity.

The Vacation That Wasn't a Vacation

Have you ever taken a vacation…and worked the whole time?

Recently, my husband and I finally made it to Grand Cayman, a trip we'd dreamed about since the pandemic. Back in lockdown, we'd unwind with margaritas, scroll beachfront real estate, and joke about ditching it all to open a bar on the beach. At the time, slinging beer to sunburned tourists felt easier than running a business during a crisis.

Fast forward five years, after a fast expansion of Exit Factor and the birth of our son, and we were finally there. No kids. Five-star resort. Ocean breeze. Frozen drink in hand: Jimmy Buffett playing "Cheeseburger in Paradise" on cue.

I'm soaking it in, sitting at the bar, and this woman next to me pops open her laptop and jumps on Zoom. No big deal, maybe it's a quick team huddle. But then comes another call. And another. Her husband's across from her, laptop open, furiously pounding out emails. Yes, they were sipping champagne and beer. Yes, they were technically in paradise. But were they really on vacation?

Not really. And truthfully, neither was I. So I picked up my margarita, moved to a quieter table, and laughed at the irony.

If you've ever told yourself, *"I'll just do a few things while I'm away,"* you're not alone. I've done it. We all have.

But that moment reminded me of something: Chuck Blakeman, in his book *Making Money Is Killing Your Business*, challenges readers to take a three-week vacation, totally unplugged. If your business can't survive without you, you don't own your business; it owns you.

That moment stuck with me.

But here's an even more uncomfortable truth: Most of us *could* take a three-week vacation, but we don't.

Not because we can't. Deep down, we don't want to let go of the tasks (and the control) that make us feel needed.

Now it's time for the next move…

Step 2: Score It and Sort It

You've mapped your role. Now, let's sort through the chaos and figure out what to let go of first.

Using your 3R, you'll give each task three simple scores:

- **Effort to Transfer** – How difficult is this to delegate?
- **Risk if Ignored** – What's the cost if it gets dropped or delayed?
- **Reward to Business** – What's the ROI if it's done well?

Each element gets a score from 1 to 3. Don't overthink this, just use your best gut instinct. Here's a grid of the scoring matrix:

SCORE	EFFORT TO TRANSFER	RISK IF IGNORED
1	Easy	Low
2	Moderate	Moderate
3	Hard	High

Once you've scored each task, we will use a quick formula to prioritize which items to remove from your plate first. (If you are using our spreadsheet, this formula, along with a color-coding system, will automatically populate for you.) The formula is:

(Risk + Reward) − Effort = Priority Score

Phase 3: Record What You Do

Ultimately, the priority score tells you what to offload first. The first things to get off your plate? Anything that is high risk, high reward, and low effort! After that:

- Tasks with scores of 4 or 5 need to be removed from your plate this year.
- Tasks scoring 3 are next in line.
- Scores of 2 or below can be saved for another year or eliminated.

Here's what that might look like based on my example from above.

ROLE/TASK	EFFORT TO TRANSFER (1-3)	RISK IF IGNORED (1-3)	REWARD TO BUSINESS (1-3)	PRIORITY
Franchisee Coaching	3	3	3	3
Management Meeting	3	3	3	3
Sales Calls	1	2	2	3
Legal Review	1	3	1	3
Client Session	2	2	2	2
Podcast Guesting	1	1	2	2
Marketing Strategy Review	3	3	3	3
Benefits Review	1	3	3	5
Updated Training Materials	1	2	2	3

Since you've mapped and scored your role, you know what needs to go. Now comes the fun, and sometimes messy, part: letting it happen. Here's how we turn a spreadsheet into strategy.

Step 3: Make the Handoff Happen

Now that you've mapped out everything you're doing, it's time to actually get you out. But here's the big question: how do you work out of these roles, strategically and sanely?

The key is first to remove ourselves from the riskiest roles in the business, based on our priority scores from above. If you are using the spreadsheet, those are areas marked by a three score. Then move down the list to the ones that have the lowest impact on risk and business operations.

You now know what to get off your plate, and when, so it's time to figure out *how* to do it. To make your handoff plan practical, we use K.A.D.E.—a tool that helps you decide what to Keep, Automate, Delegate, or Eliminate.

For every task, you want to choose one of the four K.A.D.E. outcomes below, and decide how to implement it.

K: Keep (for now)

For low-value, hard-to-hand-off tasks, or ones that are not worth the cost to delegate, yet. Just don't make it permanent. Ideally, you should complete your 3R once a quarter and remove even more stuff from your plate.

The secret that most successful entrepreneurs, CEOs, or top performers follow is that they continually re-evaluate and elevate themselves over time. If you are just starting your business, the 3R process may take years to get you to your ideal role. If you are running a larger company, you might already be half there!

A: Automate

Automate the task if a system or technology can handle it better, faster, or on autopilot.

Here's an example: Instead of manually chasing unpaid invoices, set up automated reminders for 15, 30, and 45 days. Implementing it requires a little effort upfront, but it saves hours and adds value to your business.

Artificial intelligence (AI) makes this outcome even more feasible. I don't believe AI will completely replace the workforce, but I do think it will reinvent it. I'm not sure any human is fulfilled when performing repetitive, data-driven tasks. Make you and your team more effective by utilizing AI to its full advantage. Not sure where to start? Here are some helpful tips I got from AI leader Geoff Woods in his keynote speech and book, *The AI-Driven Leader*:

If you aren't sure if AI can help, ask it! Here are some prompts:

- "This is my task; what AI tools can help me complete it?"
- "What are the pros and cons of automating this task through AI versus having a human complete it?"
- Then (and this was my biggest takeaway), have the AI tool you are using clarify your ask, to make sure it fully understands it, with this prompt:
- "Before you answer my request, please ask me up to five questions (one at a time) to ensure you understand the request. Then restate it back to me before proceeding."

D: Delegate

If someone on your team can take on a task or role, give it to them **and let them own it.** I find that working with our clients, most owners do not fully delegate tasks to a team member, and then they are upset when the work doesn't get done without their direct involvement.

I love how Mike Michalowicz explains this in *Clockwork*: "Deciding" is telling someone what to do. That still makes you the bottleneck. "Delegating" is giving ownership of the outcome and letting go.

We delegate the task, but hang onto the decisions. That's not delegation, it's disguised control. The most challenging exercise we conduct with our clients in Exit Factor is the delegation step. Many of them already have team members who can handle the tasks on their plates, but they hesitate to fully release control. Therefore, they have team members who are underutilized, not challenged, and often bored, and the owner, in turn, is burned out.

E: Eliminate

Is the task not producing results or just draining your time? Cut it. Revisit the exercise we just completed in the Optimize section related to expenses: Is it effective and necessary for your business? If not, discard it. The same applies to your tasks as well.

We had a client who was completing fifteen-minute pre-introductory Zoom call meetings before their first meeting to set expectations. What he found was that not only was the prospective client not benefiting from the time, but it also hurt his close rate. He eliminated it, freed up almost ten hours of his team's time, and increased his revenue.

K.A.D.E allows you to buy back your time and start the transferability process. However, you can't complete the exercise without the two-week time audit we discussed. If you didn't do it in Step 1, please go back and complete that step now.

Set the Handoff Plan

Now, it's time you turn this insight into action. Here's how you finalize the handoff. This is the final piece of the 3R worksheet, where you establish:

- **Who the New Owner Is**: Who's taking this over? Identify a team member, contractor, virtual assistant, or a new role you need to hire for.
- **What the Target Date Is**: When will the handoff be complete? Set it and get it on the calendar.
- **What's the Current Status**: Use simple progress markers: Planned, In Progress, or Done to track where you are.

The process doesn't have to be perfect; it's about progression. You just have to be committed. Start with one task. Then another. Then another. And watch what happens when you stop being the glue and start being the owner again.

To wrap things up, here is a look at my final transfer plan:

ROLE/TASK	K.A.D.E. STATUS	FUTURE OWNER	ROLE TITLE	TIMEFRAME TO TRANSFER	STATUS
Franchisee Coaching	Keep	Me			
Management Meeting	Keep	Me			
Sales Calls	Delegate	John	Consultant	Q4 2025	In Progress
Legal Review	Delegate	Maggy	Director of Operations	Q1 2026	Planned
Client Session	Delegate	John	Consultant	Q4 2025	In Progress

The Exit Factor

ROLE/TASK	K.A.D.E. STATUS	FUTURE OWNER	ROLE TITLE	TIMEFRAME TO TRANSFER	STATUS
Podcast Guesting	Eliminate	N/A			
Marketing Strategy Review	Keep	Me			
Benefits Review	Delegate	Chris	CEO	Q2 2026	Planned
Updated Training Materials	Delegate	Maggy	Director of Operations	Q2 2025	Completed

Think of the transfer plan as your 90-day action board. Every quarter, set aside time to review what's still on your plate, what needs to move, and what's already been completed.

While we're focused here on business activities, this exercise is equally applicable to your personal life. How much time do you spend cooking, cleaning, running errands, and managing family logistics?

I get asked all the time how I manage to do so much. The truth? I don't do it all. I've had a personal assistant through my sister, Jaclyn Poole's, company since 2015, and they've been doing my laundry, meal prepping, and running errands every week. The time I've saved is *unreal*.

Just some food for thought: what could you let go of if you stopped trying to do everything yourself?

Case Study: What One Role Can Cost You

We once worked with a dental laboratory. One of the things I love most about my job is seeing all the weird and wonderful ways people make a million dollars (or more!) in business these days.

Case in point: veneers.

Do you know how they're made? I didn't. It turns out there are two options. One, you take a mold of your teeth, and they 3D print new ones. Alternatively, if you prefer the full Rolls-Royce of veneers, you can have them hand-carved.

And if you wanted the **best** veneers in the world, the kind that looked so natural you'd swear they grew in that way, you came to our client. He was the **Picasso of veneers.**

And to his credit, he'd done a great job getting out of most of the seats in his business. He didn't handle sales or client management. He never hired or trained anyone. He had just one job left.

You guessed it: **hand-carving the teeth.**

Talk about a unicorn hire. He didn't want to carve teeth forever; he tried to exit. But he was still the product.

He eventually found a buyer for the business, but it wasn't the kind of deal the owner had hoped for. He had to seller-finance a significant portion of the purchase price and sign a five-year employment agreement.

He didn't want a job; he was in his seventies and wanted to retire!

What the buyer did on day one shouldn't surprise you. He asked the seller, "Where did you learn to hand-carve teeth like that?"

And the seller casually said,

"Oh, right down the street at the Hand Carving Teeth Institute" [or whatever it was called].

So the buyer walked down the street, met with the Dean, and asked if they'd consider creating an apprentice program.

The answer? They would love that opportunity.

Six months later, the buyer had six apprentices in training. The original owner was on track to exit within the year, and the business was worth **three times** what he paid for it.

The moral?

Yes, you are the best at something in your business. But most companies don't need a Picasso in every role. And the truth is that you can find someone to do it well enough, or even better, if you give them the chance. Holding off on transitioning roles off your plate (even your core competency) will cost you.

Delegate, Elevate, or Hire

Now that you know what needs to be removed from your plate, it's time to take action, which may involve building your team.

I get it, hiring can feel daunting. You may be concerned about payroll, margins, or whether the return on investment (ROI) will be sufficient. But **if you reallocate your time strategically, every smart hire should multiply your top and bottom lines.**

And it doesn't have to mean full-time W2s.

The gig economy has exploded with talented freelancers, virtual assistants, and contract professionals who can seamlessly integrate into your business without adding overhead.

Ask yourself:

- Do I already have a team member who could take this on?
- Can I bundle tasks to justify a part-time or full-time hire?
- Does this need to be done onsite, or can a remote contractor handle it?
- Would a freelancer or agency with specific expertise be faster and more efficient?
- Could I bring on an intern or recent grad for short-term project support?

The Boss Can't Do It All:
What Bruce Springsteen Taught Me About Letting Go

There's a good reason we hold onto control for too long: it works. It's often what made us successful in the first place.

Take my musical hero, Bruce Springsteen. He's an admitted control freak. In documentaries about him and the E Street Band, you'll see Bruce obsessing over every note, every lyric, every tiny sound in the studio. And he's notoriously the same on the road.

At live shows, you can hear him directing mid-performance: "Turn the horns up! No, turn them down!"

This wasn't a phase; it was the standard for decades.

And it's not like he didn't have someone he could delegate to. Right there, in every one of those scenes, is Steven

Van Zandt, his right-hand man, playing, producing, and orchestrating for forty years.

Bruce could have let go. But he didn't until now.

In 2024, Van Zandt was officially named Musical Director of the E Street Band. His response?

"About 40 years too late."

Most of us don't lack capable people; we've got them. What we lack is the willingness to release control.

That's not a systems issue. It's a leadership one.

Wrap-Up: From Essential to Exponential

By completing the Role Release Roadmap (3R), you're not just lightening your load: you're building a scalable, sellable, and surprisingly fun business.

Your mission is to become less essential every ninety days and watch your business become more valuable. Not because you're unimportant, but because your company deserves to thrive without handcuffs.

This isn't just theory; I've experienced it firsthand.

I have used this process in my company once a quarter for years. This exercise is how I transitioned from working over sixty hours a week in one business to owning more than 25 companies that generate over a quarter billion dollars in revenue annually. It didn't happen overnight, but it happened. And the payoff to myself, my team, and family? Massive.

You can do the same.

This process delivers freedom. Freedom to spend your time where it matters most. Freedom to elevate your business so it generates more income: for you, your team, and your family.

And most importantly, freedom to exit when you're ready, on your terms.

Case Study: Chris's 3R Plan

Since we have already walked through the exact spreadsheet in the chapter with my example, we will simply summarize Chris's results in our case study review for the Record Phase.

Step 1: Get Real About Your Role

Like most owners, Chris found himself overseeing multiple roles. He hadn't given, or didn't have, team members who took on the role entirely with decision-making authority. The primary issue we uncovered was that he was either not utilizing some team members to their maximum capacity or that he had the wrong people on his team. Here are the roles he was still sitting in:

- Sales
- Client Service/Delivery
- Operations

- Finance
- Human Resources
- Marketing

Step 2: Score It and Sort It

Based on his scoring system, he identified the roles that were most essential for him to remove himself from this year: Client Service/Delivery, Finance, and Human Resources. The problem? He already had people in those roles.

Step 3: Make the Handoff Happen

Chris decided to keep Sales, Operations, and Marketing...for now. For the Client Service/Delivery portion, he discovered that he had the wrong person on the team and needed to replace that team member. That task went on his to-do list immediately. For Human Resources and Finance, we decided to outsource to a new PEO (Professional Employer Organization) and fractional CFO firm rather than the ones he was currently using. We had identified both of those expenses as "not working" in the Optimize phase, and that, combined with the realization that he was still involved in these tasks, shed light on the fact that those companies/individuals were not pulling their weight.

The Result

The reality of the situation is that Chris had been growing his organization by continually adding more "doers" to the work serving his clients and contracts, but he was operating a very lean management team. (This situation is *very* common for growing businesses.) These quick fixes were our first step in the process to free up more of his time, allowing him to start building a professional leadership team for the organization.

Eighteen months later, Chris had stepped out of every seat, and the business was on track for its most profitable year yet, without him in the weeds. Chris's biggest unlock wasn't documenting his processes or installing a new system; it was the mindset shift. He started trusting his team, truly delegating, and stopped thinking like a founder and instead acting like an investor. And that changed everything.

Phase 3: Record What You Do

Your Move

Reflection

If I stepped away from my business for three weeks, what tasks would most likely fall through the cracks, and why are they still assigned to me?

Simple Action Step

Complete your 3R Review.

Pick an upcoming two weeks in your calendar to start documenting what you do daily. I know, it's mundane but necessary. Once it's done, use your one hour per week for Exit Factor activities to complete the 3R sheet. ***Bonus: Have your team participate in the exercise with you!***

Tool to Use

Download the **Role Release Roadmap** template at exitfactorbook.com.

This tool will guide you through the steps of the 3R system, enabling you to complete your time audit.

Chapter 7

PHASE 4: TRANSFORM YOUR GROWTH

Scale Smarter and Faster

Where We Are in the VORTEx

By now, you've done the hard part. You've cleaned up the chaos, streamlined your team, and started getting real about your role.
Your business is officially more efficient.
So now what?

Now it's time to do what most of you have been dying to do from the beginning: grow, but grow with purpose because you've done the work to earn this next step. Your patience has paid off, but we won't grow for growth's sake. I am going to **Transform** your

The Exit Factor

business and make it more valuable along the way. I'll show you how to identify your smartest growth opportunities using the **3-Growth Matrix (3GM)**—so you scale smarter, not just bigger.

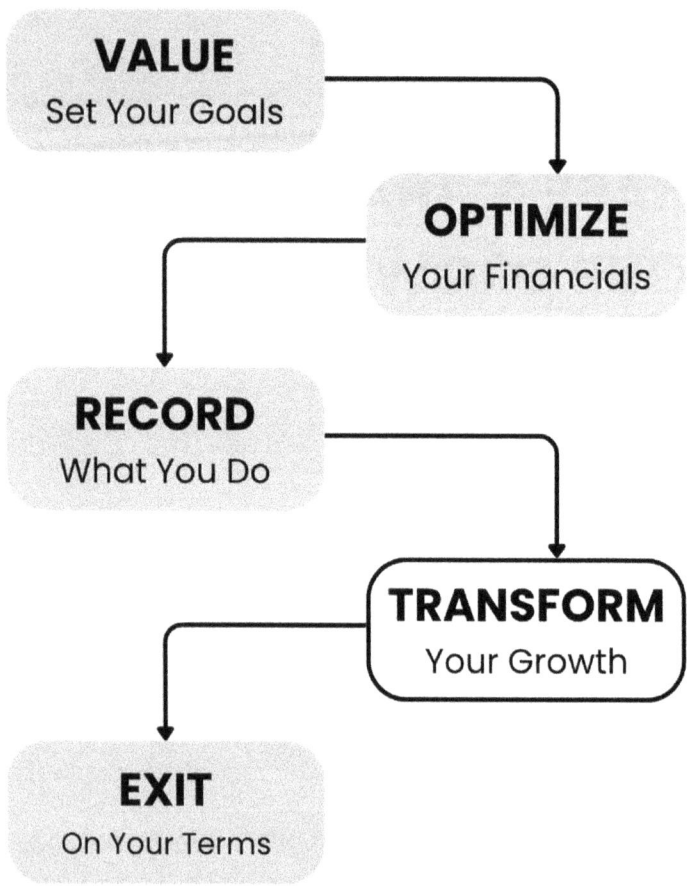

Transform is about using growth as a tool to increase value, not just to chase numbers or fill your calendar with more client work. Without boundaries, you're just adding stress, not value.

The **3-Growth Matrix** will help you stay focused. 3GM consists of three different growth levers:

- **Customer Expansion Lever** – Find and attract more of your best-fit, most profitable clients.
- **Product/Service Expansion Lever** – Offer more value to your best clients and make it easy for them to say yes again.
- **Acquisition Growth Lever** – Grow fast by buying another business, the right way.

If more than one lever looks good? Awesome. But we'll start by picking just **one** first. (Focus wins every time.)

If you're like most entrepreneurs, you've been chomping at the bit for this moment, so let's grow!

The Focus Is Still Profit Over Revenue

This lesson hit home for me in my first company, where I learned the hard way that not all growth is good growth.

In my first business, Decanted, growth was the goal, specifically, top-line revenue. We were obsessed with volume. We wanted to hit vanity numbers, qualify for larger wine allocations from suppliers, and, above all, move quickly.

So we launched what became one of our biggest hits: *The Decanted Wine Throwdown*.

It was part wine tasting, part competition. We invited our top distributors to bring their best six bottles (always with a theme), and ticket holders got to vote for a champion. It was packed—over 100 people every time, a waitlist, press coverage, word of mouth, and a crazy number of bottles flying off the shelves.

From a volume standpoint, it was a win. These were our highest *revenue* days outside of Christmas week.

But here's the dirty secret: we barely made any money.

We would discount the wines so heavily to drive case purchases that margins were razor-thin. And the events were **exhausting**. They were fun, sure, but each one took a whole weekend to recover from. It wasn't sustainable.

After about a year, we paused and asked: *What if we grew smarter, not noisier?*

We began listening to our most valued customers: the serious collectors. They didn't want to fight the crowds in a hot retail space. They knew what they wanted and preferred it to be delivered straight to their homes.

So we shifted. We stopped chasing volume and started sourcing ultra-rare, high-margin wines, such as Domaine Romanée-Conti, Screaming Eagle, and First Growth Bordeauxs. Wines with real profit and prestige. Our margins skyrocketed. Orders were prepaid. And we eliminated exhausting party planning logistics.

Were some folks sad that the Throwdowns ended? Definitely, but the business and our sanity were in a much better place.

In the end, we traded noise for value and ultimately ran a business that rewarded us, rather than draining us. That's the goal of Transform.

Why Growth Matters Even Now

Now, a few of you are still very engaged in your business and do not want to think about exiting anytime soon. You're excited about this phase!

But others, you are headed out the door, and soon. And if you're reading this thinking, *Ugh, more work?*, I get it. But Transform isn't about doing *more*, it's about doing *better*. And most of the time, smarter growth means less of *you* in the middle of it.

So you may be thinking to yourself, *Why do I have to focus on new growth opportunities? Isn't that the next owner's job?*

Fair question.

Whether you're a year away or ten, strategic growth boosts your income today and the valuation of your business tomorrow. No one wants to own a stagnant company. The next person who becomes your organization's CEO wants just as much growth as you do, and probably more. When have you ever bought an asset and been happy if the returns stayed the same?

However, let's not forget the primary focus of Exit Factor: to enhance the profitability and value of your company. So here are two rules of Transform you must follow to protect your time and value:

1. Stick to the profit bar you set in Optimize.
2. Don't add more roles and responsibilities to your plate; you just got rid of them in Record!

Any strategy must fit within those guardrails. If you're still running your quarterly "Is it working? Is it necessary?" audit, high five. That's how you find the budget to execute your growth strategies and hire the people to do it.

After decades as an entrepreneur and working with thousands of business owners, I have found that the simplest and easiest tweaks to your business result in the highest profit growth. So, let's figure out what those are in your business.

Two Roads to Growth: Which One Fits?

Now, when it comes to growing your business, there are two primary options: **organic growth** and **growth through acquisition**. First, let me explain the difference.

Organic Growth

Organic growth is the traditional, steady way to scale, which allows you to:

- Scale consistently over time.
- Feel a sense of pride and accomplishment for you and your team.
- Add one or a few customers at a time, not overwhelming your business.

It's slower, but it gives you more control. It keeps your team focused on specific, achievable goals. And let's be honest: there's real pride in growing and feeling the wins every week.

But the downside? It's slow. And while it may seem inexpensive at first, the real cost is often hidden, including lost opportunities, extensive labor hours, and delayed profits. Many business owners assume that organic growth is the safer and smarter route. But if it takes three years to hit a target you could have reached in one through acquisition…what did that extra time cost you?

Organic growth is essential, but for many, it won't close the gap between where you are and where you want to be.

Growth Through Acquisition

Acquisition, or buying another business, is the fast lane to transforming your company.

With the right deal, your business can experience overnight growth of 50% or more. You can gain instant market share, expand your products and services, attract sought-after customers, and leverage technology or resources to your advantage.

Sometimes, acquisitions even solve problems you can't fix internally. Many blue-collar industries, such as roofing and HVAC, have turned to acquisitions in recent years to address supply issues with their skilled labor pools. Instead of facing brutal hiring battles with their competitors, they have simply acquired the competition, instantly expanding their workforce.

There can also be huge financial advantages. Think about the restaurant industry: many restaurants spend hundreds of thousands, sometimes millions, on build-outs, only to have half of the restaurants fail within the first year. What happens to those brand-new, fully equipped locations? They often sell for pennies on the dollar, sometimes as little as $50,000. Savvy restaurateurs snap up these second-generation spaces, opening new locations for their brand for a fraction of the original cost.

Acquisition can also shortcut learning curves. Instead of figuring out new markets from scratch, you buy your way in with an established presence, tested systems, and traction already in place.

But with all great rewards come significant risks. Even the best, most professional buyers of businesses can fail at times.

Acquisitions come with very real challenges:

- Systems and processes don't always mesh.
- Company cultures can clash.
- Financial records can be incomplete at best or inaccurate at worst.
- Leadership redundancies can create tough staffing decisions.
- Acquiring the wrong company or too many companies can strain cash flow and divert attention from core business activities.
- And if you overpay for a business, it can hurt not just the company you buy, but also damage your existing organization.

The Deal You Don't Do Is Sometimes the Best One

Several years ago, I had the opportunity to acquire a competitor.

He'd been in the industry much longer than I had, with a well-established reputation and a name people trusted. On paper, it looked like a smart move: instant market share, a built-in client base, and less competition.

But the numbers? They stretched beyond what I was comfortable investing. And truthfully, something just felt…off. No glaring red flags, but my gut was whispering, "*Be careful.*"

Still, I couldn't shake the fear: *What if someone else buys it and starts eating into my market? What if they do it better, and put me out of business?*

That fear nearly convinced me to do a deal I knew wasn't right. Fortunately, I listened to my instincts and walked away.

About a year later, he did sell the business. And almost immediately, the team left. Most of the customers followed. The company unraveled fast.

And all I could think was: *If I had done that deal, it wouldn't have just been a bad investment, it could have taken down my entire business with it.*

A poorly timed or overpriced deal can wreck everything you've built. So, yes, acquisition is powerful, but it needs to be done with the guidance of experts and in a thoughtful manner.

So, Which Growth Path Is Right for You?

Both strategies have their place. One is steady. One is fast. Neither is "better," only better for where you are now.

That's why in the next section, we'll walk through the 3-Growth Matrix (3GM) to help you identify the best, most profitable growth path for your business **today**.

Organic Growth Options

Option 1: Customer Expansion Lever

It sounds easy. Get more customers, right? But as any entrepreneur knows, if it were that easy, we would all be running $100 million businesses. Finding the right person and convincing them to do business with your company is one of the most complex challenges in the business world. But if you know how to do it well, it's a superpower.

The Customer Expansion lever is designed to help you identify your most profitable and loyal customers and then target similar customers.

Let's walk through it step-by-step.

Step 1: Define Your Most Profitable Customer

Yes, we're starting with the basics, again. And if you're thinking, *This feels too basic. I already know who my best customers are,* trust me. Almost all of our clients have lost touch with this at some point.

Why? Because after spending years in your business, the basics get buried under a hundred other urgent fires, meetings, and distractions. When you launched your companies, you may have created customer profiles, then forgotten to revisit them and ensure they still aligned with your goals. We assume we know our best customers, but often, we don't know them deeply enough, or at all.

Take, for example, one of my clients, Sarah. She had spent nearly twenty years building her business as a personal financial coach for fixed-income older families…or so she thought. When we walked through the Customer Expansion exercise, she was shocked to realize that her most profitable and enjoyable clients weren't retirees at all. They were high-net-worth families with school-age children. In addition, almost all of them had found her through referrals from executive assistants, a referral partner she had never intentionally targeted. Once Sarah shifted her messaging and focused her marketing efforts around this ideal client, her business and valuation took off like a rocket.

Typically, when you grow your business, you likely market first and then evaluate later to see if you have reached the right individuals and had the right conversations. Think about that…it's completely backward!

First, you need to understand who the right individuals are and how to reach them. If you skip this step, you end up throwing spaghetti at the wall: burning money on marketing by chasing the wrong leads, sending the wrong messages, or, worse, doing both.

How to Do It:

Begin by compiling a list of all your customers. Sort it by profitability, who provides your company the most profit (not just revenue). Then, out of the top ten, pick three clients you love working with.

Pull out your 3-Growth Matrix (3GM) sheet and use the Customer Expansion section to answer key questions for those three clients. Here they are, as well, for ease:

Customer Avatar Deep Dive

- What industries or verticals are your clients in?
- What's their revenue range or employee count?
- Who signs the check? What's their title or background?
- Are they local, national, or global?
- Why did they come to you?
- What's keeping them up at night?
- What are their most critical outcomes or success measures?
- Where did they come from? What did they search for?
- What made them choose your company over competitors?

These questions will provide a starting point to recognize the similarities and differences among your ideal clients. But I encourage you to go deeper. If you need help, working with a coach or one of our certified Exit Factor consultants can take you further.

The more specific you get and the more precise the picture, the stronger your marketing and sales will be.

If you want to take it to the next level, consider taking those top three clients to lunch. Ask them about their life, who and what they surround themselves with, and how they make decisions.

If you can't write a two-page life story about your best customer, you're not ready to market to find more of them.

Step 2: Find Look-Alike Audiences

When you know your ideal customers, it becomes much easier to find them.

Now it's time to brainstorm new markets, channels, and partnerships. Ask yourself:

- Are there any **geographic regions** that you haven't explored yet?
- Are there **adjacent industries** with the same pain points?
- Are there **online marketing channels** where these customers already hang out?
- Could you **form strategic partnerships** to reach them faster?

This is where the "expansion" in customer expansion occurs. Don't overcomplicate it.

Just ask yourself: **Where are more of these individuals, and how can we reach them more efficiently?**

Step 3: Understand the Buying Process

Next, dig into how your ideal customers make decisions.

If you know them well, you should understand:

- What was the original problem or goal they were trying to solve?
- How did they research solutions?
- How did they find you?
- What outcomes were most important to them?
- Why did they ultimately choose you?

In the 3GM worksheet, list the primary **buying triggers** you discovered. Then ask:

> *How can I create, or capitalize on, these buying moments more often?*

Here are some examples to get you started:

COMMON BUYING TRIGGER	HOW TO LEVERAGE
Contract Renewal Season	Launch targeted email campaigns ninety days before key dates
New Product Launch	Offer bundle discounts or joint marketing partnerships
Internal Team Turnover	Position your service as stability during transitions

These triggers become the basis of your marketing message. It's not enough to find customers; you also need to use language and offers that will help them choose to work with you.

Now that you know who you are targeting, how to reach them, and what to say to them, it's time to do the hard work: execute. Draft an outreach campaign based on your knowledge, implement it, and follow the results for at least ninety days. Ensure that you include tracking metrics to measure your results and adjust the campaign for greater effectiveness.

Summary: Should You Focus on Customer Expansion?

In this phase, it's not about chasing every growth opportunity; it's about doing the **right thing** first. Your goal is to identify the growth opportunity **that is the easiest to execute and provides the highest profit increase quickly.** Once you have implemented that opportunity and reaped the benefits, it's time to move on to the next.

But how do you identify the right one first? I've included a quick self-check assessment at the end of the three levers of the

3-Growth Matrix. If you check two or more boxes for any lever, this is a strong opportunity for growth for your company.

Here is the self-check for the Customer Expansion Lever for reference:

☐ We have the capacity to serve more ideal customers.

☐ We do not fully serve our target industries.

☐ We know who we want more of, but we don't have a clear plan to find them.

Pro Tip: Increase Your Profit While You Increase Your Customers

Remember, the Transform phase isn't about getting busier. It's about getting more profitable. Go back to your profit margin bar. Do not be tempted to chase big customers or big projects at the expense of your bottom line. The wrong customers burn out your team, create churn, and erode your value.

Now that we know how to grow through customer expansion, let's take a deeper look at our products and service lines.

Option 2: Product/Service Expansion Lever

Sometimes the most efficient way to grow isn't finding more customers, it's giving your **current** ones more ways to say yes.

The founding of Exit Factor was a result of this exercise. At our mergers and acquisitions firm, we list and sell over 500 businesses annually, a record-setting achievement for the industry. However, when I reviewed our CRM in 2018, we had 1,500 conversations with business owners who said, *"I love what you do, but I'm not ready to exit my company yet."* Over three times the number of conversations we had were with clients who weren't attracted to our primary service but wanted to do business with us in the future. I asked myself, *"How can we help those customers now?"*

The Product/Service Expansion lever is about doing exactly that: expanding or optimizing what you offer to **increase revenue per customer and grow your margins** while providing another service that your customers need or desire.

Here's a secret: your customers want fewer vendors, not more. They want partners that offer more. This secret is how Amazon became so successful. Jeff Bezos and his team figured out early on that households don't want to order online from ten companies to get basic supplies. They prefer one provider, one account. You don't need to be as big and diversified as Amazon, but most businesses have untapped opportunities sitting right in front of them:

- Add-on services customers have been asking about.
- Create premium versions of core offerings.
- Offer downsells or upsells that expand the customer's journey with you.

Step 1: Audit Your Current Offerings

Before you expand, you need to know what's working and what's not. For most of us, we probably don't have enough products or services; we have a product concentration issue, which means that 80% or more of our revenue comes from one core product line. We need to expand our offerings so we are not too reliant on our core.

> ### *Case Study: How Many Soaps Do You Have?*
>
> For some of you, you may have too many products. One of our clients developed a custom skincare line specifically for pregnant women. She had built a loyal cult following and was generating almost one million in revenue when sales and profits began to fall dramatically. When we first met and toured her facility, I immediately knew why. The warehouse was packed to the roof with boxes, and tables had formulas and mixes spread all over.
>
> I looked at her and said, *"How many SKUs (products) do you have?"*
>
> *"500."* Over 500 products for a business that was not yet seven figures. No wonder sales and profits were crushed, and we hadn't even looked at cash and debt yet. She had been spending so much time creating and expanding, sinking her energy and money into new products, that she hadn't stopped to think about what was producing the best results.

And the worst part? That strong following of clients dwindled **because they were overwhelmed and confused.** Buyers of all products and services want simplicity. We already have too many options, especially for new pregnant women and new moms: please just tell us exactly what to buy...I don't want to scroll!

If you find yourself in the opposite situation, where you have a large number of products generating minimal revenue, it's time to cut, not expand. Doing so will boost your revenue, profit, and value.

Analyze your results

Go to your 3GM worksheet and list each product or service, scoring it on three dimensions: the percentage of your revenue each product generates, the average profit margin for the product or service, and the customer satisfaction rating (low, medium, or high). Here is an example:

PRODUCT/ SERVICE	REVENUE %	MARGIN %	CUSTOMER SATISFACTION
Product A	15%	65%	Medium
Product B	10%	20%	Low
Product C	75%	50%	High

You're looking for trends here. Some offerings may carry the business. Others may drain resources or attract the wrong customers. Review your findings and decide which products or services to focus on and which to discontinue. For example, Product B in the chart above not only provides a low revenue percentage but also delivers a lower margin and customer satisfaction rating. This business owner would be better suited to expand upon Product A than divert their attention to Product B.

Product C is their winner. It provides a high customer satisfaction and a good margin. However, they are highly dependent on it, as it accounts for 75% of their revenue. This product presents an excellent opportunity for the business to expand its C product line and increase growth while diversifying its revenue risk.

Step 2: Identify Gaps and Opportunities

Now, flip the lens: what do your customers *wish* you offered?

You don't need magic for this exercise. You often find clues if you listen to your customers and take note of their:

- Frequently asked questions.
- Common complaints.
- Recurring requests for upgrades, add-ons, customizations, or faster service.

Opportunities may also lie within your team. If you have a sales team, ask them what types of questions or requests they get when selling or servicing their customers. Look for opportunities to expand the features and offers of Product C.

Which of these opportunities apply to your products?

- ☐ Add-ons that customers regularly request.

- ☐ Premium or VIP versions of existing services.

- ☐ Faster delivery or "done-for-you" options.

- ☐ Support, education, or training that enhances results.

Based on the feedback, brainstorm a list of ideas that you could use to expand your product or service line.

Step 3: Build Your Product Path™

Now it's time to put your research into action. This exercise isn't about adding more. It's about adding **better**, only after auditing what's already working.

Ultimately, you want to build your Product Path: a journey that allows customers to start small, fall in love with your brand, and naturally deepen the relationship over time.

Most customers won't buy your most expensive offering right away. But once they trust you? They will want to buy more. Returning to the Amazon example, the first purchase you made from the website probably wasn't a big-screen television. But after a few book purchases, toilet paper, and snacks, you think nothing of having a TV show up on your doorstep.

Using what you learned in the last two steps, sketch two to three potential packages or tiering ideas for your business. Think good → better → best.

Here's a quick example from our company, Exit Factor:

PACKAGE/ SERVICE NAME	WHAT'S INCLUDED	PRICE	VALUE
Book	Basic overview of the Exit Factor Program	$	Core concepts to provide a DIY experience.
Exit Assessment	Customized assessment of business value and plan	$$	A value growth roadmap tailored to the customer's company.
1:1 Consulting	Hands-on coaching to execute a customized roadmap	$$$-$$$$	Direct implementation support for maximum results.

Now, it's your turn. Start with the winning product you already have (like Product C, shown in step 1). Is that your good, better, or best option? How can you create an upgrade or downgrade from that product or service? Use your brainstorming list from step 2 to help. Finally, make an upgrade based on the same list. This process isn't about adding fluff. It's about smart tiers based on your collected customer feedback that inspire customers to choose the best option for themselves, while allowing you to maximize revenue and value.

Summary: Is Product/Service Expansion Right for You?

It's time to return to that self-check to help you identify whether this growth lever is the opportunity you should pursue for your business.

If you check **two or more boxes**, Product/Service Expansion may be the lever that unlocks the fastest, most profitable growth.

☐ Our customers are asking for more than what we offer.

☐ We don't have a way for customers to engage further with us if they want.

☐ We have extra resources or capabilities that we aren't leveraging.

Is Recurring Revenue Real or Hype?

You've probably heard the term "recurring revenue" tossed around like it's the holy grail. And it can be. But what is it exactly?

Recurring revenue refers to **predictable, ongoing income** that is consistent and reliable, recurring year after year.

That doesn't mean you have to launch a membership model (although you can). It's about establishing a baseline level of predictable income every year.

Developing your Product Path can be a solution for that recurring revenue. Within your Product Path, you can build in models like:

- Memberships or subscriptions
- Renewable contracts
- Service clubs or loyalty programs

But if you don't have a Product Path yet? Start there. Get the foundation right before layering in anything else.

Phase 4: Transform Your Growth

As mentioned, every business needs a form of organic growth, so I recommend choosing one of the options we already covered: customer expansion or product expansion. However, some of you will also need a second type of growth, one we explore next: growth through acquisition.

Option 3: Acquisition Growth

Growth through acquisition can feel like a daunting move, but when executed correctly, it's one of the fastest and most effective ways to scale.

Whether you acquire a competitor, a vendor, a company in a neighboring market, or even just a database or customer list, you're buying years of growth you don't have to build from scratch. You gain new customers, talent, established systems, and a stronger market position…all in one night.

Medium Player to Market Dominance in One Week

An established sign company had been in business for ten years but struggled to compete with a larger player in town. No matter what the owner did, the other guy just seemed to be a step ahead of him.

One day, he heard from a friend that his competitor was retiring and looking to sell the business. He jumped at the chance and moved quickly. Within a week, he had the company under contract and a closing scheduled.

> Fast forward six years, and now he doesn't just dominate his market but has grown to be one of the biggest and most valuable sign companies in the state, something that would not have been possible without that acquisition. The market power he gained also accelerated his organic growth, and there is still more for him to expand.

But this lever comes with real risks. That's why I will walk you through it carefully: so you can evaluate whether you're ready, identify where the opportunity lies, and move forward wisely.

Step 1: Evaluate Strategic Fit

First, consider what kind of acquisition would make the most significant impact for you.

I find it helpful to ask yourself the following questions about your business:

- Are there any competitors I can acquire?
- Where do I currently refer business out?
- What is my most significant constraint?
- What are my largest expenses?
- Who already has my ideal customers?
- Is there a vendor or customer in my supply chain that complements our business?
- Is there a new market I want to enter?
- What capabilities are holding us back?

One of our clients ran a business generating approximately $300,000 in EBITDA when they identified a perfect acquisition opportunity: an underperforming competitor generating $200,000 in profit. They bought the company for $600,000, merged operations, and instantly grew to $500,000 in EBITDA, jumping their valuation from a 3x to a 5x multiple almost overnight. After one year of running the VORTEx Model, EBITDA increased by an additional 50%, and the company's value rose to over $4.5 million. Strategic acquisition didn't just grow their business; it multiplied their exit value by more than 400%.

The goal here is not to acquire just for fear or ego, remember my story about the competitor I didn't buy? The right deal should provide you with a strategic advantage, allowing you to expand quickly into an area that would otherwise take years to achieve.

Step 2: Assess Financial Readiness

This next step is where many owners either get stuck or take reckless action.

Let's clear up a myth that's spreading like wildfire.

If you've spent any time online, you've probably seen the "zero-money-down" crowd: those influencers and so-called gurus promising you can buy a business with no money, no experience, and no risk. Sounds impressive, right?

That's because it's designed to hook you. Those influencers are not giving you real-world advice; they are stealing your attention to sell you expensive courses.

The truth is that successful acquisitions require capital, financing, and time. Do you need millions in the bank? No. However, you do need to invest some of your own money, bring relevant experience to the table, and be prepared to commit real time, often a year or more, to finding and integrating the right deal.

Even professional buyers (and these influencers) aren't doing deals the way they claim because that's not how it works in the real world.

The chart below outlines the range of financial, funding, and time requirements. Assess your financial situation to determine if you can afford an acquisition. The chart is also included in your 3GM worksheet.

NEED	DESCRIPTION	YOUR ASSESSMENT
Free cash available to invest	Most acquisitions require a 10-30% cash down payment, plus additional out-of-pocket expenses such as search fees, accounting, and legal fees.	
Financing	Lending programs, such as the SBA 7(a) loan, can fund most small- to mid-sized acquisitions. You will need good credit and a relationship with an SBA bank.	
Time available before your exit	Plan on at least 6 months to find and close on an acquisition, plus 1-3 months to stabilize integration before your ultimate exit.	

Phase 4: Transform Your Growth

Remember: you're not just buying a business, you're buying the integration process. That costs time, money, and leadership attention. The wrong acquisition or the acquisition at the wrong time can distract you from your core business opportunities.

When Acquisitions Go Sideways

James owned a profitable IT services firm with a reputation for customized support for mid-sized businesses. After a decade of steady growth, James decided it was time to take the next step.

When a neighboring company, a SaaS product company, came up for sale, it looked like the perfect shortcut to faster growth.

He moved fast and bought the company. However, after closing, cracks emerged. The two companies had completely different business models and customer bases.

Although his main company was solid, James was still heavily involved in the sales process. And when he split his focus trying to integrate the business, his grasp on his core clients slipped.

Exaggerating the issues, James had already put himself in a cash crunch, using most of his cash

> reserve for the acquisition, along with using a loan guaranteed against his assets for the remainder. When the sales dipped, he had no savings to fall back on.
>
> When James tried to sell the combined companies two years later, his options were limited. Both businesses had declining revenue and profit, the kiss of death for any business valuation, and buyers didn't feel like breaking them apart or trying to fix them. In the end, James sold for far less than he could have *and* was still paying off the acquisition loan.

Step 3: Snapshot the Risk and Reward

Finally, let's map out the upside and the real risks involved with an acquisition.

Here's a simple model to decide whether acquisition is the right fit for you. It is already mapped out with a couple of examples, but you can use the blank 3GM worksheet from exitfactorbook.com to do your assessment.

If you want to acquire a competitor, the potential rewards include additional revenue, clients, or team members. However, there are also associated risks, most commonly related to integration issues or losing your financial investment. There are ways to mitigate these risks, but it's best to create and map those strategies before the deal happens, not after.

OPPORTUNITY	POTENTIAL REWARD	RISK	MITIGATION STRATEGY
Acquire a local competitor	$1M in added revenue	Poor integration = investment loss	Retain key staff; have seller transition accounts
Expand into a new market	2 new territories	Core business distraction	Ensure the acquired company has a leadership team in place; pilot before full rollout

If this lever is a viable option, enter it with your eyes wide open and a lot of help. Don't rely on gurus; hire a real team of experts instead. You will need a broker or investment banker, a mergers/acquisitions attorney, and an accountant fluent in acquisitions of your size (they don't need to be an expert in your industry, but that's a soap box of mine for another chapter).

Sam Zell's Simple Filter for Big Decisions

If you're struggling with how to grow or making any significant decision, this simple filter is helpful. Sam Zell, one of the most successful investors of all time, had a simple three-question test before he ever made a move:

- What's the upside?
- What's the downside?
- How do I protect against the downside?

That philosophy enabled him to become a billionaire across various sectors, including real estate, energy, logistics, and manufacturing. Zell didn't just make a wild bet on opportunities; he built downside protection into every deal he made.

Before you pursue any acquisition or major project, channel your inner Zell, because growing fast is fun. Losing it all? Not so much.

Summary: Is Acquisition Your Best Growth Lever?

Let's be real: Acquisition is a longer-term play. **You need at least three years before your planned exit** to make it worthwhile.

Professional buyers know a secret (and now you do too): **the first year after an acquisition, the acquired company's performance is often flat or down.** No matter how strong the target company is, change shakes things up. It takes time for teams, customers, and systems to adjust, and for the full return on investment to show up.

With that in mind, do a self-check:

☐ We have at least three full years before our planned exit.

☐ We have the financial strength and lending options to fund it.

☐ We have the leadership and team capacity to absorb another company.

With this lever, you must have **all three components** to move forward with an acquisition strategy.

Now it's time to choose which lever of the 3-Growth Matrix (3GM) is the best for you to pursue first, keeping in mind that you are seeking transformation that's both easy and profitable.

Which Growth Lever Should You Pull?

LEVER	BEST FOR	KEY ACTIVITIES	BIGGEST BENEFIT	RISKS
Customer Expansion	Businesses that have untapped markets of customers	Define your ideal customer, find lookalikes, and leverage buying triggers	Low-risk growth using what already works	Not well-defining your ideal audience, wasting money on marketing dollars
Product or Service Expansion	Businesses with strong customer relationships and room to increase lifetime value	Audit your offers, identify gaps, and build your Product Path	Higher revenue per client leads to better retention	Overly complex offers or cannibalizing existing products or services
Growth Through Acquisition	Well-run businesses with strong systems and financial stability	Find a strategic fit, assess your financial readiness, and develop a risk-reward plan	Fast growth, market-entry, talent acquisition	Integration risk, culture clashes, and overpaying for the acquisition

The Concorde: When Innovation Isn't Enough

In the 1970s, the Concorde was the pinnacle of aviation achievement. Sleek, fast, futuristic, this supersonic passenger jet could fly from New York to Paris in just over three hours. That's faster than most people get through TSA today.

With its needle-nose design, luxurious service, and the ability to cruise at twice the speed of sound, the Concorde wasn't just fast. It was iconic.

Until it wasn't.

By 2003, the Concorde was officially retired. Not because it stopped working. Not because it wasn't still, in many ways, extraordinary. But it couldn't sustain itself.

It was too loud. Too expensive to operate. Too fuel-inefficient. The tickets were astronomically priced, yet the airline lost money on every flight. It was an engineering marvel. But a business disaster.

Here's the lesson:

Sometimes the best innovation is not the best business model.

I often see this in the entrepreneurial world: founders who've created something impressive, maybe even industry-defining, but the numbers don't work behind the curtain. Margins are razor-thin. Systems are messy. The business is running at full throttle, yet it is still bleeding cash.

In the Transform phase, this becomes even more critical. Because no matter how "cool" your business looks from the outside, buyers will dig into the engines. They'll look at cost structures, profitability, and efficiency. And if it doesn't fly without burning through fuel and cash? They'll walk away or offer you much less than you expected. Don't focus on the growth opportunity that will garner the most likes or traffic. Focus on the opportunity that will provide the most profit and value.

Wrap-Up: Transform for Value, Not Just Volume

You've made it through the most exciting, and, for most, the fun, phase of the Exit Factor program: Transform.

Transformation is about **profitable growth**, designed to boost your exit value, increase your income now, and create real leverage in your business.

Each path works. But each one may not be right, right now, in your business. Select the one that best fits your goals, capacity, and timeline.

Case Study: Chris's 3GM Plan

I'm going to walk you through Chris's 3-Growth Matrix Plan and how he ultimately decided which lever was right for his business.

Customer Expansion:
- ☐ We have the capacity to serve more ideal customers.
  Yes! This part was exciting. Chris found that while they were swamped, they were too busy servicing customers they didn't enjoy working with and not spending enough time and energy with the ones they loved.
- ☐ We do not fully serve our target industries.
  Yes! If they focused on their identified ideal client, there were plenty more to serve.
- ☐ We know who we want more of, but we don't have a clear plan to find them.
  Yes! The customer expansion exercise was helpful, and now they are ready to create a plan.

Product or Service Expansion:
- ☐ Our customers are asking for more than what we offer.
  No. Chris's customers were not asking for any more; if anything, they seemed overwhelmed.

- ☐ We don't have a way for customers to engage further with us if they want.

  No. *They had numerous opportunities for clients to engage further, but few were taking advantage of them.*
- ☐ We have extra resources or capabilities that we aren't leveraging.

  No. *The team's resources were exhausted entirely, and they were all burned out.*

Growth Through Acquisition:

- ☐ We have at least three full years before our planned exit.

  No. *Chris wanted to be out of the business within the next two years at the latest.*
- ☐ We have the financial strength and lending options to fund it.

  No. *The company was already cash-strapped and could not afford any more debt.*
- ☐ We have the leadership and team capacity to absorb another company.

  No. *Although Chris delegated more to his leadership team in Phase 3: Record, he was unable to take on another company.*

The Best Growth Lever for Chris's business right now is Customer Expansion.

Outcome:

The customer expansion exercise was life-changing for Chris. He finally realized that those big customers were sucking him dry. Not only were they unprofitable, but the team also disliked working with them. The demanding clients also pulled Chris's team into services that they weren't skilled at or didn't enjoy, so they ended up outsourcing some of the work for even lower margins. All in, when Chris and his consultant finalized the results of their research, the top two clients were costing Chris $250,000 per year.

Ultimately, he let them go. This move allowed Chris to refocus his energy on his ideal target client and what they loved doing: strategic project work.

By firing his biggest clients, Chris saved $250K, kept his best team members, and doubled down on what made the business both fun and valuable again. The team was happier, and so was the bottom line.

Phase 4: Transform Your Growth

Your Move

Reflection

Which growth lever offers the highest profit with the least effort, and why haven't we pulled it yet?

Simple Action Step

Now that you've explored all three levers, it's time to choose your focus. It's far better to pursue one growth path, execute it well, and then move on to the next, rather than juggling multiple strategies simultaneously. Select the lever that offers the highest return on investment (ROI) with the lowest complexity for your current situation.

Tool to Use

Download the **3-Growth Matrix (3GM)** template at exitfactorbook.com. This tool will guide you through the three different levers for growth and help you identify which is the best for your company.

Choose Your Lever:
- ☐ Customer Expansion: "We need more of our best clients."
- ☐ Product/Service Expansion: "We're leaving money on the table with current clients."
- ☐ Acquisition: "We're ready to grow big, fast—with the right deal."

You can revisit the other levers later. But for now? Commit to one. Because at the end of the day, Execution beats multitasking every time.

Chapter 8

PHASE 5: EXIT, BUT NOT THE END

Scale Smarter and Faster

Where We Are in the VORTEx

You've thought about exiting. Maybe after a hard day. Maybe with a glass of wine in hand. Now it's time to prepare.

This is the moment we've been building toward. If you've followed the program, you've created real value, and now it's time to cash in on it, on your terms. Whether that's one year or ten years from now, how you exit will be one of the most significant moves of your life.

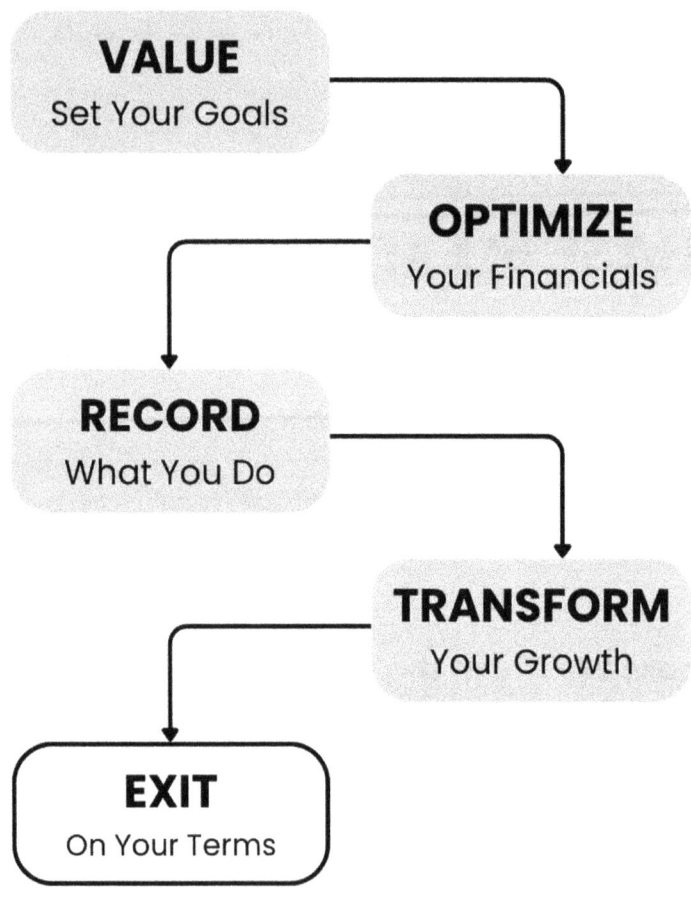

Phase 5: Exit, But Not the End

In this chapter, we'll walk you through the Exit Prep Scorecard (XPS), your tool for choosing a clear exit path, assessing your readiness, and assembling your team.

> **Get The Exit Prep Scorecard (XPS)**
> **from exitfactorbook.com**
> Grab your **Exit Prep Scorecard** at exitfactorbook.com. As we walk through each path, reflect on your top option, your fallback, and the advisors you'll need to make it happen.

This scorecard helps you:

- Define your primary and backup exit paths.
- Identify your most probable buyer.
- Evaluate your readiness across key factors.
- Build your transition team.

Let's walk through what your scorecard will guide you to do, and how your choices intersect with the genuine buyers in today's market.

Our first stop is to revisit and finalize your exit options. As we discussed previously, there are five primary ways business owners exit. Let's walk through each one in more detail and discuss how to determine which path is right for you.

The Business Was Never the Dream

Joe spent nearly twenty years building a powerhouse hair-care brand, developing innovative products, cultivating a loyal online following, and establishing a reputation that stretched nationwide. Although he built something significant, he was, well, exhausted.

When he sold the business for a life-changing sum, he expected to feel a sense of relief. Instead, he felt…lost.

Then he remembered the dream he'd buried decades ago.

Long before formulations and fulfillment centers, Joe had been a singer. A cappella, to be exact. It was his first love, one he never fully let go of, but hadn't been able to enjoy for decades. So with his calendar finally clear, he auditioned. Got in. And for two years, he toured the country with a professional vocal group, bringing his dream to reality.

Building the business gave him success. Letting go of it gave him *back* his purpose.

Now it's time for us to do the same for you.

Step 1: Choose Your Primary Exit Path

Your first task in this phase is to determine which type of exit aligns best with your personal, financial, and lifestyle goals. People love to say, "You need a plan." But the vast majority of plans fail to survive their first contact with real life. What do you really need? Options. And a framework to choose the right one when the time comes.

Every business should have an option they are aiming for (primary exit target) and a backup plan in case the original plan goes off the rails.

Here are the five main exit options available to you. I gave a quick overview in Phase 1: Value, but now we will cover them in

Phase 5: Exit, But Not the End

more depth, including what type(s) of buyers you deal with in each option and a bit about their psychology.

There's no perfect path, but there is a best fit for *you*. Here's a quick look at the trade-offs:

EXIT OPTION	PROS	CONS	BEST FOR
Selling to a Third Party	Highest payout potential	Requires strong valuation and prep work	Owners wanting liquidity
Family Transition	Legacy, continuity	Emotionally complex	Owners with willing heirs
Employee Ownership	Continuity, culture alignment	Risk of fallout if mishandled	Businesses with strong internal leadership
Hire CEO/ Retain Ownership	Retain equity, long-term income	Requires complete trust and release	Owners still passionate about their business
Structured Dissolution	Clean break, potentially tax-advantaged	No legacy continuation	Business is in trouble with no clear buyer or successor

Option 1: Selling to a Third Party

This is the option most people imagine when they think about exiting: selling to someone outside their organization for a big check, starting a new chapter, and enjoying a champagne toast. And yes, it can deliver the biggest payday. But it only works if your business is truly ready.

Common third-party buyers include:

- **Strategic and Synergistic buyers** – competitors or other similar businesses looking to expand their market share.
- **Investment buyers** – growth-focused investors like Private Equity, looking for 3–5x returns.
- **Individual buyers** – seeking their next career opportunity or investment.

When considering a third-party sale, you need to prepare your company for due diligence, an extensive inspection process of a business. The due diligence process is why we have done so much work through the VORTEx Model. Your financial records, legal documents, and operational processes will be scrutinized.

Although most owners start with another exit option in mind, a third-party sale is typically one of the most frequent options that business owners choose.

One of our clients had three PE firms circling with offers to buy their business. Because her business ran smoothly without her and her systems were well-organized, she didn't just choose the highest-priced offer; she selected the one that aligned with her team's culture. The power of the preparation process lies in the options it provides.

Phase 5: Exit, But Not the End

Let's look at each of these buyer groups for a third-party sale more thoroughly:

Strategic and Synergistic Buyers
- **Who They Are:** Your competitors or companies in related industries looking for synergies.
- **What They Want:** Growth through acquisition, expansion of the customer base, and increased market share.
- **Top 3 Deal Killers:**
    1. Poor alignment with their existing operations.
    2. Lack of scalable systems.
    3. Unclear financial performance.

Investment Buyers
- **Who They Are:** Private equity firms, family offices, or search funds with investor backing.
- **What They Want:** High EBITDA (minimum of $500,000 or more), a leadership team in place, and a clear growth path.
- **Top 3 Deal Killers:**
    1. Low or inconsistent earnings.
    2. Lack of a management team.
    3. Complex or opaque financial records.

Individual Buyers
- **Who They Are:** Corporate escapees, entrepreneurs through acquisition, or past business owners getting back in the game.
- **What They Want:** Proven cash flow, manageable operations, growth potential.

- **Top 3 Deal Killers:**
    1. High owner dependence.
    2. Messy or unclear financials.
    3. Lack of transition support.

Sara Blakely: Scaling Smart, Exiting Strong

Selling to a third party can be the ultimate reward for building a truly valuable business, and no one embodies this better than Sara Blakely, founder of Spanx.

Sarah disrupted an industry and built a billion-dollar company from her bootstraps. When she launched Spanx in 2000, she had $5,000 in savings, no fashion experience, and no investors. But she had a brilliant idea: to create comfortable shapewear that women would want to wear.

From day one, Sarah prioritized profitability. She didn't take on investors who would demand rapid scaling or control. Instead, she built lean, maintaining ownership while growing through wise, intentional choices.

The most remarkable part? She designed Spanx to run without her. By hiring strategically and building a strong culture, Blakely ensured that Spanx didn't depend on her showing up daily. Sarah's favorite role in the company was not even CEO. She spent most of her time on design, research, and development, and instead hired professionals to handle the other aspects of managing the business. This move made the company highly attractive to potential investors and buyers.

In 2021, when Sarah decided to sell a majority stake to Blackstone for a reported $1.2 billion, it wasn't out of necessity or burnout; it was a strategic choice. She still owned 100% of the company at the time of sale. And because she had kept control, she could thank her employees with cash bonuses and two first-class plane tickets to anywhere in the world.

Her exit wasn't forced or rushed. It was the culmination of years of intentional scaling and strategic ownership.

Selling to a third party can be a strategic win if you build your business right. Like Sara Blakely, you can scale smart, exit strong, and choose how and when to walk away.

Now that we know more about a third-party sale and who we are selling to, is this your preferred exit option? If so, I highly encourage you to read my first book, *Getting the Most for Selling Your Business*, where I cover the topic in more detail.

Option 2: Transition to Family

A lot of business owners dream of passing the torch to a child, a sibling, or another family member: someone who's been around the business dinner table for years. It feels like the most natural exit.

With this option, there is more than just business dynamics; it is personal, and regardless of the outcome, it will impact your family. How you treat the exit will determine whether it is a positive or negative experience. Some generations leave the business and need to be compensated for the company, while their children wish to inherit it. For most founders and entrepreneurs, gifting is often not an option; they need the sale value or ongoing salary to fund their next phase of life.

According to Cornell University's Smith Family Business Initiative, only 40% of family businesses make it to the second generation, 13% to the third generation, and a mere 3% survive beyond the third generation. In my experience, these numbers are dwindling; fewer second and third generations have been interested in carrying on the family business in recent years.

Take John, for example. He built an $8 million raw materials business from the ground up, with twenty employees and decades of sacrifice.

His son, fresh off business school, seemed like the perfect heir. But they'd never actually talked about it. Over Thanksgiving dinner, John dropped the bomb: *"I'm retiring in January. You'll take over and pay me a lump sum and an annual salary."*

His son said no. He had other plans.

The business was shuttered ten days before Christmas. Twenty jobs were lost. A father-son relationship was fractured, and regret lingered even decades later.

Phase 5: Exit, But Not the End

The lesson? Don't just assume someone wants your business, even if they are a family member.

Some items that need to be addressed include:

- Identify suitable successors.
- Discuss the succession of the business.
- Establish a mentor, training, and gradual transition plan to prepare them for ownership.
- Establish a firm plan, including a timeline and clear expectations for exit value.

Hermès: When Family and Tradition Go Right

Now, let's talk about the opposite of John's story. If there's one brand I admire most, it's Hermès. Founded in 1837, the brand started as a harness workshop in Paris, crafting high-quality leather goods for European nobility. Nearly 190 years later, it remains one of the world's most iconic luxury brands and is still family-controlled.

You may know Hermès from their beautiful leather goods and iconic orange boxes, but the story you probably don't know is one of the fiercest dedications to family loyalty and legacy of any company.

In the early 2010s, the company faced a significant threat. LVMH, the world's largest luxury conglomerate, began quietly buying shares, aiming to absorb Hermès into its empire. Alarmed, the Hermès family, more than fifty descendants strong at that point, decided they weren't about to let a mega-corporation dictate the future of their storied brand.

They came together and contributed their shares to a holding company, H51, and legally bound themselves to each other for a minimum of twenty years. They agreed that no matter what, those shares would not be sold. This unified front not only blocked the takeover but also reaffirmed the family's dedication to preserving Hermès' independent spirit and legacy. Recently, the family just renewed H51's charter for another ten years. You have to commend a family that, in the face of all of them becoming millionaires if not billionaires, stands together in support of their legacy and gives the finger to their acquirers.

Your business might not be Hermès, but the principle still applies: when families align around shared values, a legacy is built. But it takes clear agreements, firm boundaries, and a shared commitment to the future, not just nostalgia.

Family Buyers
- **Who They Are:** Family members or close associates considered successors, often already involved in the business.
- **What They Want:** Legacy preservation, gradual transition, clear roles and expectations.
- **Top 3 Deal Killers:**
    1. Assumed interest without confirmation (not all next-gen members want the business).
    2. Conflicting expectations around ownership versus management roles.
    3. Lack of communication regarding the financial terms of the transition.

There is only one key to success with this transition: communication. Too many family businesses fail to communicate effectively and frequently about how the transition between generations will occur.

Option 3: Sell to Your Team (Without It Blowing Up)

Selling your business to your team might feel like the most loyal move you can make. After all, they've been with you through thick and thin.

Selling the business to an employee or group of employees is called a management buyout (MBO). These exits aren't casual agreements. They're real transactions with lawyers, funding requirements, and leadership handoffs.

However, only about 9–10% of the population is entrepreneurial, so most of your employees do not want to own a business! We once worked with an owner who was willing to give (free of charge) a multi-million-dollar business to his leadership team. The team said no because they did not want the risk, and instead, they encouraged him to sell. Once sold, the owner gave each of them a bonus, and they all continued to work in the business for the new owner. Just like family transitions, discussion with your team members is key; most of them are not willing to take on the risks of owning a business.

But in the right circumstances, when the management team is committed to the business's continued success, this can be an excellent exit option. In an MBO, the sale can be completed through a standard or structured sale over time or through an employee stock ownership plan (ESOP).

There are risks to selling to employees. I've seen certain situations where an owner believes the best and only path to exit is through a management buyout and approaches the employees first. However, if that deal does not come to fruition, the employees now know that the owner is shopping the business for sale and may decide to leave the company.

An owner of a training company assumed his leadership team would want to buy the company. Everyone had been there for years. They were loyal, talented, and emotionally invested. However, when the deal structure was finalized, with real money and absolute personal guarantees, every single one of them backed out. Two left the company immediately and started their own competing business. The exit fell apart, and the owner tried to recover but was devastated. Eighteen months later, he sold what was left for $220,000, down from an initial value of $3.5 million.

The lesson? A management buyout sounds appealing, but it's not always what your team wants. Always prepare multiple exit options, and never assume interest means commitment.

Phase 5: Exit, But Not the End

Management Buyers
- **Who They Are:** Longtime employees, managers, or the entire employee base.
- **They Seek:** Stability, a gradual handover, and fair financing terms with minimal risk.
- **Top 3 Deal Killers:**
    1. Unrealistic valuation.
    2. Unclear leadership transition.
    3. Lack of financing options.

What's All the Hype About ESOPs?

If you know me, you know my love for Wawa runs deep. I've dined at some of the world's finest restaurants, three-Michelin-star spots where plates are practically works of art. But final meal? There's no question: a Wawa hoagie, turkey and provolone, dry, lettuce, tomato, pickles, salt, pepper, and oregano, with a side of mashed potatoes and a diet half and half. Call it basic if you want, but you can take the girl out of Jersey, not the Jersey out of the girl.

However, Wawa isn't just the best hoagie joint on the planet; it's also one of the most successful examples of employee ownership in the U.S.

Founded in 1964 as a dairy market in Pennsylvania, Wawa has grown into a chain of over 1,000 convenience stores along the East Coast.

As Wawa expanded in the early 2000s, the owners faced a critical question: How could they keep growing without losing their culture? The answer: Employee Stock Ownership Plan (ESOP). Instead of risking the brand's soul by selling out or going public, Wawa made its employees co-owners. The result was workers who aren't just making sandwiches but are making investments in their future.

Employee ownership gave Wawa's team a genuine stake in the game, which is evident. Employees take pride in the store's success because they own a stake in it. Plus, it's hard to hate your job when your retirement plan hinges on how well you make a turkey hoagie.

The bottom line is that Wawa's ESOP didn't just preserve the brand; it amplified it. Employees stay longer, work harder, and treat customers better. ESOPs typically only fit large organizations with expansive payrolls and are complex to execute. But when do they work? It can be a magical solution to an exit.

Not every great team makes a great buyer. But if you have exemplary leadership in place, there's another option…

Option 4: Step Back—Hire a CEO

An exit does not have to end with a sale. Some founders still love the business but not the grind that comes with it. If that's you, this path might be your sweet spot. Instead of selling, you step back and let someone else manage the day-to-day operations. You become the owner. The investor. The board chair. But not the operator.

The key to this exit strategy is being willing to walk away.

You can't hire someone to lead and then hover over them. If you're still in meetings or signing off on every PO, you're not out; you're just micromanaging from a new seat. It's like hiring a babysitter then hiding behind the couch to eavesdrop the whole night.

You may review financial statements quarterly, show up to board meetings, and evaluate whether to divest or reinvest more money in the future…that's it.

One of our clients brought in a brilliant COO-turned-CEO. The first six months were rocky, not because of the CEO but because the founder kept intervening. Once he finally pulled back, profits grew 18% year-over-year, and his team morale shot up. The bottleneck had been…him.

This exit is an entirely different process that falls outside the scope of this book. But in general, you will need to:

- Design the CEO's job role.
- Identify the ideal candidate's qualities.
- Utilize a high-quality sourcing party to help recruit candidates.
- Employ an intensive hiring process, including management and peer interviews.
- Institute an onboarding phase.
- Execute a transition phase where each of you operates in tandem for a short period.
- Hand over the reins and step back, allowing the new CEO to lead the organization independently.

Now, let's move to the last option.

Option 5: Orderly Dissolution (a Strategic Close)

Not every business ends with a big exit, and that's okay. Sometimes, the cleanest and healthiest move you can make is to shut it down with intention. No shame. No drama.

Going out of business is the exit option most business owners choose; as you know, almost 87% of companies in the United States close their doors. And in some cases, it's the only option. However, there is a distinction between owners who happen to go out of business and those who plan to do so. Planning to go out of business, also called a structured dissolution or orderly liquidation, is a strategic exit option for business owners.

It can allow them to wind down their company in a controlled and tax-efficient manner that may produce more liquidity than the other options we have discussed. Through a structured dissolution, the company's assets are sold, debts are paid off, and any remaining proceeds are distributed to the owner or shareholders.

Think of it like harvesting the garden before winter. You gather what's valuable, straighten the ground, and create space for what's next.

If this option interests you, see if there is a way to sell your business for assets only (both tangible and intangible).

- A business broker may be able to help with this, OR
- One of your competitors may be willing to acquire some or all of your assets, even if it is just your inventory and database.

- If an asset sale is not viable, reduce your inventory through a going-out-of-business sale.
- Sell your equipment to equipment dealers or competitors, AND
- Sell your database.
  - Active and maintained databases can be valuable. You can structure a deal with your competitors to:
    - Pay you upfront for your database, OR
    - Pay you a commission over time from revenue generated (also known as an earnout).

Please consult with your accountant before executing any sale or reduction of assets to ensure that you can accurately capture it on your taxes and reduce your tax payment owed.

Going out of business strategically sometimes can net more cash than a traditional sale.

If you choose this path, do so with your eyes open and your head held high. A clear ending can be a powerful beginning.

Choose Your Path—and Own It

Now that you've seen the landscape, one or two paths probably feel right. Use the Exit Prep Scorecard (XPS) and refer back to your Value Vision Map (VVM) from Chapter 4 to determine which path aligns with your vision, timeline, and current state of readiness.

The choice is yours, but the key is to select a primary exit option and then plan accordingly. Once you have chosen your option, the next step is to design the roadmap and timeline. The roadmap will largely depend not only on your exit but also on the end goal. That goal is based on:

- How much exit value do you want out of the business—either sales, transition price, or profitability from ownership?
- When do you plan to exit the business?
- How much time and energy do you have left to devote to the plan?

And here's the good news: the option you choose today doesn't have to be forever. The goal isn't a rigid plan. You can pivot later because you'll be prepared either way.

Grab your XPS and evaluate each exit option above by answering the prompts, and then select the one that is your primary exit option. Here is a copy of the XPS exit option chart below for your reference:

EXIT OPTION	IS THIS YOU?	CIRCLE ONE
Sell to a Third Party	You want to cash out, step away, or move on to your next venture.	Yes / No
Transition to Family	You want to preserve the legacy and keep it in the family.	Yes / No
Sell to the Internal Team	You want your team to take over and succeed you.	Yes / No
Hire a CEO and Keep Equity	You want recurring income but less day-to-day involvement.	Yes / No
Orderly Dissolution	The business is in trouble; you don't have the energy to invest in fixing it, but you want to extract value.	Yes / No

Phase 5: Exit, But Not the End

If You're Not the CEO, Then Who Are You?

Now you know your exit options. Logically, it's straightforward. But emotionally, it's a shift most owners underestimate.

Because stepping back or letting go isn't just a strategic move; it's an identity shift. And that can be scary.

Back in the Value chapter, you took time to imagine your Inspiring Future, not your business's future, but yours.

That vision wasn't just an exercise. It was a glimpse of what's waiting on the other side of your exit: a version of your life where time, freedom, purpose, and peace are finally possible.

So now I want to ask you:
- What does life look like if you're not the CEO?
- What scares you most about stepping away?
- What are you still holding onto that no longer serves you?
- And if you had the time, the money, and the space, would you finally step into that future you imagined?

This moment, the decision to let go, isn't about loss. It's about making room for the life you said you wanted. But if you haven't addressed the feelings and changes you are about to go through, you could subconsciously sabotage all your hard work to prepare for this exit in this final phase.

Step 2: The Importance of a Backup Plan

The second step of the XPS is selecting your backup plan. Let's be real; very few exits go precisely as planned. Buyers back out, markets shift, and team members get cold feet. That's why successful entrepreneurs don't just plan; they prepare. Remember Sam Zell's mantra: What's the upside? What's the downside? And how do I protect myself against the downside? That means having a backup.

Pick one or two fallback options you'd be open to if your ideal path doesn't go as planned, and identify them on your XPS worksheet in Step 2.

Consider what would need to happen for each to become viable, and list the necessary conditions that must be met. That way, you're not scrambling if your Plan A hits a wall; you're pivoting with purpose.

Backup Option	What Would Need to Happen to Make This Work?
_____	_____
_____	_____

Even the best-laid plans can fall through. By preparing your backup options now, you're giving yourself the freedom to pivot without losing momentum or money.

Think of it like having a storm shelter. You hope you never need it, but if the winds shift, you'll be glad it's there.

> **Quick warning:** A backup plan isn't just a wish. It has to be executable.
>
> What if your fallback is "sell to employees," but your team doesn't want ownership? That's not a plan—it's a trap.
>
> Choose options you can act on.

Step 3: Build the Team to Make It Happen

No matter your chosen exit path, you'll need a strong team to execute it. The right experts can mean the difference between a smooth transition and a chaotic one. In the next step of the Exit Prep Scorecard, we identify the players you need on your team.

An Overview of the Players

Now that we've identified your primary exit option and backup options, we need to work on setting you up for the actual exit execution process. The first step in this process is building the right team. Based on research by the Exit Planning Institute, when an exit goes wrong, 85% of the reason is that the wrong team, or no team, was involved. You have put in the hard work; don't skip the critical step of building your team of experts and specialists to bring you to the finish line.

The Exit Factor

ROLE	WHAT THEY DO
Exit Execution	Your main deal quarterback could be a business broker, investment banker, or ESOP advisor. They market the business, manage negotiations, and keep the deal moving.
Tax Team	Designs a deal structure that minimizes taxes and avoids costly surprises. Ideally, it includes both a proactive CPA and a tax attorney.
Legal Team	Handles contracts, due diligence, and entity structure. You need more than your general business attorney; this is exit-specific.
Wealth Manager	Helps you prepare for life after the sale. Think portfolio planning, asset protection, and legacy building. The earlier they're involved, the better.

Exit Execution

Depending on your exit option and the size of your business, you will hire a business broker, investment banker, or ESOP specialist to quarterback your deal.

Phase 5: Exit, But Not the End

If you sell your company for less than $30 million, you will typically engage a business broker or M&A advisor; for those above $30 million, an investment banker is generally used.

If you plan on selling your company to your employees through an ESOP, you will need a specialist to complete the transaction.

Regardless of the party, this person or firm serves as the quarterback of the transaction, with the primary responsibility of coordinating all other individuals involved, including legal and tax representation. They may recommend using partners in these areas, but you should always conduct your own interviews and make final selections yourself. Besides quarterbacking the deal, their job is to *sell* the company. This job is broken into the following steps that they must complete to make that happen:

- Prepare the business for the sale process.
- Find and qualify buyers.
- "Sell" the business.
- Negotiate the terms of the deal.
- Quarterback due diligence.
- Manage the pre-closing process.

One of the Biggest Myths of Exits: I Need an Industry Specialist

When I'm working with clients approaching exits, they all start down the same path: "I have to work with a team of advisors who are specialists in my industry." And the thought, while well-intended, could not be further from the truth.

If you look at the most talented deal makers in the world, they all have one surprising skill in common: they are unbelievably creative. And that creativity stems from being involved in hundreds of business sales over the years across multiple industries.

Think of it this way: if you need heart surgery, you don't go to a general practitioner; you go to a heart surgeon. But you don't need that heart surgeon to specialize in treating 5'7" women of Italian descent. You want an experienced M&A advisor, not necessarily a lifer in your industry.

Business brokers who specialize in a single core industry can be narrow-minded, with thoughts like this is how deals are done in this industry. There is no standard way to do a deal in any industry. Every single deal and company is different, and that's why you need a creative advisor on your side.

Worse yet, many industry experts tend to work with the same core buyer group repeatedly. Which raises my concern: Where is their fiduciary responsibility? Is it to ensure their client, the seller, gets the best deal possible? Or is it to ensure that their long-term relationships with their buyers are not affected?

Sometimes, business owners want to skip this role. I may be biased in this belief because I come from an M&A advisory background, but even if I were to sell my own companies, I would hire a broker or investment banker rather than doing it myself.

One of the most significant changes in the last decade for entrepreneurs has been the overwhelming number of exit "offers" that face us. If your company generates more than $1 million in annual revenue and has more than five W-2 employees, you are likely to receive solicitations to sell your business regularly. I hate being the one to burst your bubble, but these companies are not interested in buying *you.*

Here's the secret pioneered by private equity firms and now adopted by every entrepreneur through acquisition (ETA for short) in the game. They:

- Purchased a list of businesses with a specific revenue size and employee count in their targeted industries.
- Used marketing software to customize the outreach to each owner.
- Sent the same email out to thousands of business owners.

The goal? To try to convince you to sell to them *before they have to compete with other buyers.* They don't want you to hire a business broker or investment banker because if you do, that person will almost assuredly create competition for your company, and the buyer will have to pay a higher price (on average, 20-30% more).

When a good business like yours goes to market, there are often 100-400 buyers or more who inquire about that business. Not just one.

Now, if you plan to use the other exit options like selling to employees (not through an ESOP), transitioning to family, hiring a CEO, or completing an organized dissolution, you will likely not need this role to complete your exit.

Tax Professionals

Next is your tax team. This team could include an accountant, a bookkeeper, and even a tax attorney or specialist. This role should be involved from the beginning, as we've discussed the importance of proper accounting and bookkeeping.

The right tax team can differentiate between a sellable and an unsellable company. When it comes time for your exit, your company will be scrutinized by rooms of individuals, including buyers, bankers, attorneys, and other certified public accountants (CPAs). It's during this time that your company needs to be run **better than ever before**, especially when it comes to financial reports.

Additionally, if you are worried about how much you will pay in taxes for your exit, this team can help you present and execute tax reduction and deferral options.

Taxes are one of the most overlooked and expensive aspects of the exit. Yes, I know you have paid (a lot) of taxes along the way of owning your business, but you will pay them again on your exit, and they are not insignificant. Your tax professionals should help you understand the tax implications of the sale and explore options to minimize the tax bill. If your team is not advising you on multiple options to mitigate this expense, you are working with the wrong team.

The right team can save you millions. Here's an example of how.

Case Study: The $1.8 Million Mistake That Almost Happened

One of our clients owned a successful SaaS business operating as a C corporation for nearly fifteen years. After years of hard work, he finally received an offer to sell the company at a price well above market value. Naturally, he was thrilled.

But there was a catch.

The buyer proposed an asset sale, not a stock sale. That might not sound like a big deal, but from a tax perspective, it was a massive undertaking. Here's why:

Two different methods for selling a business exist: stock and asset sales.

- A stock sale allows the business owner to pay capital gains tax on the proceeds, which is typically lower than the tax on other types of income.

- An asset sale requires the owner to pay a mix of capital gains and ordinary income tax; in some cases, that combination can be brutally high.

The tricky part is that almost all small business sales are asset sales, which provide better legal protection for the buyer.

But in his case, the difference between the two approaches was staggering. If the deal were to proceed as an asset sale, he would face a combined federal and state tax rate of 65% on the sale.

But, as a C-corp in the SaaS industry, his business was approved as a Qualified Small Business Stock (QSBS) under Section 1202 of the Internal Revenue Code. That meant if he structured the deal as a stock sale, he could pay 0% federal capital gains tax on the increased equity value. In other words, he'd keep far more of his hard-earned money.

Fortunately, we brought this up early in the process, and he qualified the business with a tax expert before the deal went through. The result? Instead of paying 65% tax on the original offer, he saved $1.8 million simply by having the right team and foresight.

Not having the proper guidance almost cost him millions. This is why having a team that understands the intricacies of your business structure and the tax implications of different exit strategies is essential.

Legal

Your attorney isn't just here to review contracts; they're your deal bodyguard. A good one protects your interests, negotiates terms that truly serve you, and keeps your dream exit from turning into a legal nightmare.

In these complex transactions, your general business attorney or friend who is a litigator won't cut it. This job is for a specialist, someone who lives and breathes deals, not just helped you set up your LLC ten years ago.

You'll want an M&A (mergers and acquisitions) attorney or a firm with proven experience on the sell side of transactions in your size range. If you're selling a company in the $3–10M range, don't hire someone whose last deal was a billion-dollar buyout.

Your legal team is responsible for negotiating, drafting, and finalizing the legal components of your business exit. They can enter the deal at any time, but no later than once you receive an offer on the business.

Here's what an experienced legal team will typically cover:

- **Letter of Intent (LOI)** terms – including exclusivity, deal timeline, and structure.
- **Purchase Agreement** – the main contract, spelling out what's included, how much you're paid, and when.
- **Employment and Non-Compete Agreements** – essential if you're staying on post-sale or protecting proprietary knowledge.
- **Due Diligence Coordination** – making sure you're only handing over the info you're legally obligated to in a secure and structured way.

- **Reps and Warranties** – those "I promise this is true" clauses that, if written wrong, can cost you big.

An excellent legal team will spot issues *before* they become problems. Consider having them conduct a "mock legal diligence review" six months before going to market. It gives you time to clean things up before buyers find them first. Refer to the bonus on the Exit Prep Scorecard for helpful insights into legal aspects, including clauses to watch out for.

Wealth Manager

A seasoned wealth advisor isn't just for "after the deal." The best ones come in early to help you preserve your proceeds, minimize taxes, and align your exit with your values. And yes, this is where the alphabet soup of acronyms shows up. But don't worry. You don't have to use all of these tools. You just need to spend some time with your advisor to identify the right one to use to accomplish your goals.

In general, the wealth manager's responsibilities are:

- Establish personal goals.
- Provide tax mitigation strategies.
- Preserve income and wealth.

Now, I'm not a licensed financial planner, and by no means is the below investment advice, but these are just some of the options I've seen clients utilize to mitigate or reduce taxes over the years.

You can use these tools to move assets, reduce estate tax exposure, and maximize your flexibility before a deal is inked:

- **GRAT** (Grantor Retained Annuity Trust): Helps shift future appreciation out of your estate.
- **FLP** (Family Limited Partnership): Consolidates assets and enables discounted gift giving.
- **IDGT** (Intentionally Defective Grantor Trust): Transfers assets while freezing their value for estate tax purposes.
- **Lifetime Gifting Strategies**: Transfer wealth to heirs tax-efficiently before your valuation spikes post-sale.

Additionally, if giving back is part of your post-exit plan, you'd prefer to give dollars to causes rather than to the IRS, you can implement some of these options:

- **CRT** (Charitable Remainder Trust): Provides income to you now and a gift to charity later.
- **DAF** (Donor-Advised Fund): Set aside charitable funds now and decide where they go over time.
- **Private Foundation**: A more hands-on philanthropic vehicle: higher cost, but more control.

Lastly, this list of opportunities can help you manage and grow your proceeds while protecting against lawsuits, taxes, or unfavorable market conditions:

- **QOF** (Qualified Opportunity Fund): Reinvest gains into underdeveloped areas and defer or reduce capital gains tax.
- **Roth IRA Conversions**: Shift tax-deferred savings into tax-free accounts when your income temporarily drops.

- **Structured Settlements**: Spread out your payout over time for tax smoothing and peace of mind.

Most owners have never heard of half these strategies, and that's okay. Your job isn't to become a wealth advisor. Your job is to build the right team early so they can design a financial strategy that protects your freedom, your wealth, and your next chapter.

> A warning here: not all wealth advisors are created equal, and just because your advisor isn't familiar with one of these options does not mean they don't exist. Also, many of these options take one or multiple years to set up before you can even bring your business to market.

Finalizing Your Team

You've now got a clear understanding of the key players involved in a successful exit. The next step? Choosing who belongs on *your* team.

At this stage, you don't need to know exactly which individuals or firms you'll work with, but you should be thinking about the functions your exit will require. Who needs to be in your corner to guide, protect, and advocate for you throughout this process?

Go back to your XPS worksheet and, for each of the roles we've discussed, ask yourself:

- Do I need this role for *my* exit?
- Do I already know someone who could fill this role?
- What qualities or experience are most important to me in this relationship?

Remember, the people on your team don't just impact your timeline or your valuation; they shape your experience. Choose partners who respect your vision, speak your language, and make you feel like you're in capable hands.

If you need help identifying trusted professionals, our certified Exit Factor consultants have a vetted network of specialists across a wide range of industries. We'd be happy to help you build the right team for your journey.

Advisor Red Flags

You have invested decades of your life in this business and now a significant amount of time in preparing it for the next phase (at the very least, the time it has taken you to read this book). Selecting the right team can solidify your exit and put more money in your pocket. But choosing the wrong team? It can kill your deal at best and, at worst, render your business unappealing to potential buyers.

If your advisor says any of these…run. Seriously.

WHAT THEY SAY	WHY IT'S A PROBLEM
"We'll figure taxes out later."	No, you won't. The deal structure is the tax plan. Wait too long, and you'll miss critical savings.
"You don't need a separate tax attorney."	Tax law is complex and expensive to get wrong. This is not the time for shortcuts.
"Let's wait until there's an offer before hiring a broker."	A good broker adds value before the offer phase by creating competition and bringing in multiple buyers to increase the offer.
"I've done M&A deals, but not recently."	Changes abound in the exit process. You need your advisors to have both depth and recent experience.
"It's not worth checking on tax savings; you probably won't qualify."	Maybe. Maybe not. But any advisor who doesn't check leaves money on the table.
"Just trust me, we don't need to include your spouse/partner."	No. You need complete alignment with the people who the sale will impact. Full stop.
"That wealth planning stuff can wait until after closing."	Actually, no, it can't. Some of the most potent tools only work years before the deal is done.
"Deals only take a few weeks."	Nope. Most take months, even a year. Any advisor selling speed over strategy is selling you short.
"Brokers/attorneys/ etc. are too expensive; you can just do it yourself."	You get what you pay for. Are the most expensive advisors guaranteed to produce the best result? No, but the best dealmakers are experienced and creative, and they are worth their weight in gold.

You've spent years building this business. Don't hand over your exit to someone who isn't qualified, or worse, isn't invested in your future.

You Built This. Now Own Your Exit.

You made it. You did the work. You faced the hard truths, dug into the numbers, clarified your goals, and built something profitable and valuable. That's no small feat. Most business owners spend their entire careers running on autopilot, hoping that someday they'll just "figure it out."

But not you. You took the time to *think strategically*, to see the bigger picture, and to take ownership of your business and your future. You chose to build with intention, to create something that not only works for you but also works without you.

That's the real win. Because now, whether you decide to sell next year, hire a CEO to run it for you, or just enjoy your business as a more hands-off owner, you have something that *can stand on its own*.

And yes, that deserves to be celebrated. Not just because you've made it to the end of this book (though that's impressive, too) but because you've chosen to take control of your destiny. You didn't settle for just being busy; you made a plan to be *free*.

But here's the thing: building value isn't a one-time decision; it's a continuous commitment. Now that you have the tools and the mindset, it's time to make your plan *real*. In the next chapter, we will break it down into **your 90-day action plan**.

This is where your vision becomes reality: you put everything you've learned into practice. We'll map out the most critical next steps, set clear priorities, and ensure you know precisely how to get from here to your ideal exit.

Do it on your terms, whether you're selling, scaling, or stepping back. You've done the hard part; now it's time to turn that hard work into lasting success.

Case Study: Chris's Exit Prep Scorecard

Now, let's return to Chris. After eighteen months of work, he finally reached the Exit phase, and what he decided may surprise you!

Step 1: Primary Target Exit
Chris came in wanting out. After the time spent building value and aligning the team, he made a pivot. He didn't want to sell anymore; he had fallen in love with the business again. He hired a CEO, retained his equity, and built a bench of trusted advisors in case he needed to change course again.

Primary Target Exit: Hire a CEO.
Ideal Candidate: Past CRO, COO, or President of a logistics company with at least $10 million in annual revenue.

Step 2: Backup Option
With the work he put in, he knew the company was sellable, not just from instinct but verified with his team of outside advisors.

Backup Option: Sell to a third party.
Ideal Buyer: Strategic competitor or individual.

Step 3: Build Your Team
Even though his backup option was to sell the company, Chris found value in building a bench of advisors that he could lean on now and in the future.

Exit and Growth Strategist: He maintained a quarterly review with his certified Exit Factor consultant to ensure they were on track with the company's valuation and exit options.

M&A Advisor: Chris selected an M&A advisory firm in his area, specializing in working with business owners in his revenue category in case of a third-party exit.

M&A Attorney: He also retained a multi-functional law firm that had attorneys specializing in both employment law and mergers and acquisitions. They also had a tax specialist on staff, in case he needed one in the future.

Bookkeeper and CPA: Chris did an excellent job selecting a bookkeeping and accounting firm in the Optimize phase and decided they would be the perfect fit to keep through exit.

Wealth Manager: However, his legacy financial planner was no longer meeting his needs. At the advice of his exit strategist, he interviewed several others and finally hired someone who worked with business owners through exits, having a multitude of resources at his disposal.

Your Move

Reflection
Do I feel ready for an Exit?

Simple Action Step
Complete your **Exit Prep Scorecard (XPS)** and revisit your **Value Vision Map (VVM)**.

Now that you have completed the entire **VORTEx Model**, it's time to select your primary exit, backup option, ideal buyer, and team. Once you have solidified your options, it's time to take action.

Tool to Use

Download the **Exit Prep Scorecard** at exitfactorbook.com.

SECTION THREE

IMPLEMENTATION GUIDE

Chapter 9

THE NEXT 90 DAYS

Turn Your Exit Plan into Motion

This Isn't the End, It's Your Beginning

If you've made it to this chapter, you've already done what most business owners don't: you've gotten serious about your exit. You've clarified what you want, why you want it, and how you're going to get there. Now, it's time to start building real momentum.

> **Mindset Reset: Your Solo CEO Retreat**
>
> Before diving into the next 90 days, pause and take a step back. Most owners don't move forward because they lack

> clarity, not capability. For me, this looks like a one-day, one-night solo retreat.
>
> Use this time to clarify what you want, where your business stands now, and what your personal goal looks like. Before you move forward with your next 90 days, schedule a solo retreat to clarify what you want.
>
> Will others think it's weird if you take yourself on a retreat? Yes, my in-laws think I'm going crazy when I do this. But believe me, the reset time is invaluable.

The next 90 days are where strategy turns into action. And no matter where you are in the process, this chapter gives you a clear, doable plan based on your timeline.

Choose the track that best describes where you are:

- **Track A:** You're not ready to exit anytime soon, but you want to build value.
- **Track B:** You're 3–5 years out. You need to build value, reduce reliance, and prep the engine.
- **Track C:** You're within 1–3 years. It's go-time; you need to prep for an actual exit.

And remember you can always visit exitfactorbook.com to get all the tools and resources (including this 90-Day Action Plan) to help you along the way.

Track A – Focus on Value and Optimization

This plan is designed to help you establish the fundamentals of profit, time, and freedom in your business, positioning you to exit for the highest dollar amount, regardless of what happens. And even if you don't exit, you can run a company that delivers more time, money, and freedom to you. Not every tool from the book is covered here, but these are the core fundamentals to put in place based on your goal.

Month 1: Reignite Your Vision

Outcome: Identify certain areas of your Vision Value Map.

Do This:
Complete these sections of the Value Vision Map:
- **Step 2: Identify your most important outcomes**
  - Even though you are not ready to exit now, what are you building your business for?
- **Step 5: Identify your primary exit and backup plan**
  - Identify your primary exit option.
  - Identify your backup option.
  - Revisit this annually.
- **Step 6: Identify your value and future needs**
  - The primary reason business owners are dissatisfied with their exit is that they feel they left money on the table. The reason that happens is because entrepreneurs aren't clear on three things up front:
    1. What is your business worth today?
    2. What is the future potential value of the company?
    3. What will the next phase of life cost you?

In order to avoid this, you can:
- Get or update your Personal Financial Plan.
- Get a professional Exit Assessment completed for your company.

> If you want a quick checkup on your business before you dive into a whole project, you can schedule time with one of our team members to review your business at exitfactorbook.com.

30-Day Mindset Check:
Are you putting off these first few tasks because:
- You are still too busy to focus on these essential items?
- It feels like you have all the time in the world?

How to Execute:
This is a heavy first 30 days, I know. Honestly, the most challenging part with these first steps and getting started is *you* and what defining you want. Use your Solo CEO Retreat (see the Mindset Reset box above) to complete your Value Vision Map.

Month 2: Profit Checkup, Part 1
Outcome: Begin the Profit Pulse Plan

Most owners hit burnout for three reasons: the business takes too much time away from the things and those they love, the company doesn't provide them enough money, or both. In these first 90 days, we want to ensure that you don't encounter any financial difficulties.

As a reminder from early chapters, the goal for any business is to make a healthy profit for its owners.

Do This:

This month, I want you to complete these parts of the PPP:

- Step 1: Where are you now?
- Step 2: Complete the "Is it working? Is it necessary?" exercise I explained in Chapter 5 for your largest expense category.

60-Day Mindset Check:

Where is your business leaking the most value?

How to Execute:

For this exercise you will need two financial reports:

- Trailing 12-Month Summarized Profit and Loss
- Go to your accounting software and locate the Profit and Loss statements. Change the date filter to "Custom" and then select the last 12 months of completed financials. Additionally, it is helpful to export these reports in Excel rather than PDF.
- Trailing 12-Month Detailed Profit and Loss
- Set the date for the last 12 months. You definitely want to export this as an Excel document.

Month 3: Profit Checkup, Part 2
Outcome: Finish the Profit Pulse Plan

This month, you will complete the "Is it working? Is it necessary?" exercise for the rest of your large expense categories. Hopefully you identified a number of expenses last month that aren't necessary to your business.

Do This:
I want you to do the work to:
- Cancel or eliminate the expenses,
- Replace the vendor or provider, or
- Fix what's not working about the expense

Now that you have lower total expenses, calculate your EBITDA margin (as a reminder, this is done by dividing EBITDA by Gross Revenue). This is your temporary profit bar, which you cannot go below. Do not add any more expenses until your revenue grows.

90-Day Mindset Check:
What quick fixes can you implement this month to eliminate profit leaks?

How to Execute:
This part is simple, but not easy. Make the decisions, and cut what's needed!

Track B – Value, Optimization, and Record

This plan is designed for those who have decided to exit but also want to invest the effort and time to do it right.

This track may feel slow at first, but that is intentional.

Month 1: Reground Your Vision, Part 1
Outcome: Begin the Value Vision Map

It is crucial at this phase that you have all the necessary foundational information to develop an exit plan that yields the best outcomes for your business and personal goals. Taking the time to do the Value Vision Map justice means not doing it all at once.

Do This:

In this first month, I want you to do two things:

1. **Start with your Solo CEO Retreat (see the Mindset Reset box above) to identify your goals.**

    Whip out your Value Vision Map and complete the following sections:
    - Creating your inspiring future.
    - Identifying your most important outcome.
    - Completing the reverse timeline and picking an exit date.
    - Identifying your primary exit option and backup options.

2. **Select two key advisors who can help create your roadmap.**

    Two key advisors who will be critical to your exit success: a wealth manager/financial planner and an exit strategist. You can review Chapter 8 again for guidance on selecting the best advisors.

30-Day Mindset Check:
If your business stayed exactly the same for the next three years, how would you feel?

How to Execute:
You are now embarking on a journey, probably the most important of your career. You need to dedicate time to it. Set aside one hour per week in your calendar to focus on your exit strategy. The key is to treat it just like you would a meeting with your most important client: don't move it, don't skip it, and don't ignore it. What gets scheduled gets done.

Month 2: Reground Your Vision, Part 2
Outcome: Finish the Value Vision Map

At this point, you should know where you want to go. Now, we need to retrieve the data to ensure we can proceed.

Do This:
Using the two advisors you selected last month:

- **Get a professional Exit Assessment completed for your company.**
  - This is no longer an optional step. You need to ensure that you understand the precise targets your business must achieve to reach its future goals. If you have selected an exit strategist from month one, this is typically the first step in working with them.

A True Exit Assessment vs. an Exit Estimate

Don't settle for an estimated value of your company's worth. Many of your advisors may be able to produce that estimate for you: an accountant, a broker, or even a financial advisor. But at this point in your journey, you don't just want to know what average companies exit for in your industry; you need to know what your company will exit for. Although a free estimate may sound appealing, it could be hundreds of thousands (or millions) of dollars off. Starting out with the wrong information for your plan is truly a recipe for failure.

- **Complete your financial plan.**
  - Likewise, now that you have a great financial advisor on your team, you need to meet with them to update your personal financial plan.
- **Update the Value Vision Map (Step 6).**
  - You should now have an idea of your wealth goal, the current value of your company, and its potential future value. These numbers will indicate whether a gap exists. Sometimes, the company you operate today will not get you to your wealth goal. That is okay! It may be a stepping stone to something bigger. You can leverage the exit from this company to help you buy or start something with even more potential.

60-Day Mindset Check:
Do you have all the information you need to understand your current business situation?

How to Execute:
You will need to set aside time in advance to get these items completed this month. That means scheduling a meeting (which could be lengthy) for your financial advisor to interview you and gain a comprehensive understanding of your future goals and current situation. Likewise, your exit strategist will need some of your time (and information).

Month 3: Start Recording

Outcome: Track your time with the Role Release Roadmap

I want to jump ahead a phase briefly to find you some more time to work on the program ahead.

Do This:
Spend your two most normal weeks this month taking a Role Inventory using the Role Release Roadmap. From there, take a look at each of your individual tasks and decide which are the lowest priority, and choose to:

- Automate,
- Delegate, or
- Eliminate.

You are not aiming to complete the full 3R this month; the goal is to find 2–5 extra hours per week that you can redirect to the processes in this program.

90-Day Mindset Check:

How much progress could you make in your business if you have two extra hours per week working on it?

How to Execute:

Track everything you do from the time you wake up until you go to bed for two weeks. Document your activities, including a description and estimated time to complete, in the 3R. Then, review the list and select a few tasks that will give you 2–5 hours back in your week. Now, get rid of them. Preparing your company for exit may not be urgent right now, but it is important, and you need to make it a priority in your schedule!

Track C – Value and Exit

So, maybe after reading this book, or even before, you've thought to yourself, *this is it, I'm done*. It's okay if you've realized that you've reached your current business's limits and are ready to move on. If so, this is the plan I recommend you tackle over the next 90 days to make your business exit as fruitful as possible.

Month 1: Value

Outcome: Identify certain areas of your Vision Value Map

Do This:
- **Step 1: Identify your inspiring future**
  - The next year you embark on (yes, this exit will probably take you a year) is hard and scary at times. You need a positive outcome to focus on, a target that

makes all of the ups and downs worthwhile. This is your inspiring future.
- **Step 2: Identify your most important outcomes**
  - You are about to enter into multiple periods of negotiation, no matter what type of exit you decide on. In all negotiations, you cannot win on all points. Knowing your most important outcome and ensuring that it remains your focus will help you feel satisfied with your exit.
- **Step 5: Identify your primary exit option and backup plan**
  - Decide which type of exit you are going to pursue, but also what your backup plan will be if that does not happen. Spend some time planning what would trigger your backup option: would it be a time frame or a monetary amount?

30-Day Mindset Check:
What outcome, one year from now, would make you feel satisfied with your exit?

How to Execute:
Use your Solo CEO Retreat (see the Mindset Reset box earlier in this chapter) to complete this.

Month 2: Assemble Your Team

Outcome: Build your team with the Exit Prep Scorecard

In order to give yourself the best chance of success with a short-term exit, you need a rockstar team.

Do This:

Here is the order I would proceed in:

1. **Exit Execution:** Select either a business broker (under $5 million in value), M&A advisor ($5-30 million), or investment banker (over $30 million) if you are selling your business. If you are proceeding with an ESOP, you need an ESOP specialist. If you selected one of the other exit options, you may not need this role.
2. **Transaction/M&A Attorney**
3. **Accountant**

Optional roles, depending on your situation, may include tax attorney, legal industry specialist, or family business advisor.

> Selecting the right team is something I'm very passionate about. Because of that, even though my company does not offer these transactional services, it is important to me that we provide support to business owners who feel overwhelmed in this program.
>
> If you need help selecting advisors, our team of certified Exit Factor consultants can assist you at no or minimal expense. Go to <u>exitfactorbook.com</u> for more information.

60-Day Mindset Check:
Are the people advising you helping you reach your goals—or just telling you what you want to hear?

How to Execute:
You should interview at least two professionals in each category before making the right selection for yourself. You can find them by asking current advisors or friends for referrals, searching the internet, or even utilizing industry association boards. No matter how many interviews you hold, give yourself a deadline to make a decision. The worst decision is putting this off.

Month 3: Prepare Yourself

Outcome: Activate your Exit and educate yourself

It's time to proceed with your exit. You have 9 months (or less) left in your exit process, and you need to activate everything you have prepared.

Do This:
For the first couple of months of the exit process, it may feel like things are moving slowly. Use this time to educate yourself about the process you are in and prepare for the negotiations ahead. Here are some additional book recommendations I have for you during this process:

> *Getting the Most for Selling Your Business,* Jessica Fialkovich
> *Closing the Deal,* Andrew Cagnetta
> *Never Split the Difference,* Chris Voss

90-Day Mindset Check:
What could derail your deal personally during this process?

How to Execute:
It's time to do everything you've been building toward. Activate your exit and run your business better than ever!

> ### Should You DIY or Call in a Guide?
> Some owners love rolling up their sleeves and handling everything themselves. Others prefer a trusted advisor in their corner to save time, reduce stress, and avoid expensive mistakes.
>
> As you move into exit execution, ask yourself:
> - Do I have the time and energy to manage this program while still running the business?
> - Am I confident in navigating negotiations, due diligence, and buyer relationships?
> - Have I led a deal of this complexity before—or do I want someone who has?
>
> If you answered "no" to one or more, you might benefit from having a certified Exit Factor consultant walk alongside you. We've helped thousands of owners like you prepare, market, and close successful exits—and we'd be honored to support yours.
>
> Learn more or get matched with a certified consultant at exitfactorbook.com.

Final Thoughts: Moving Forward

This plan is just the start. If you commit to this plan, you'll find that the freedom you've been chasing will start to take shape. You'll feel more in control, more prepared, and, most importantly, more aligned with the life you want to lead.

Don't wait until you're forced to make big decisions under pressure. Schedule your solo retreat now—even a half day—to check in, reflect, and plan. The exit is inevitable. Your power lies in how prepared you are for it.

What to Do in the Next 10 Minutes:

- Pick a Track
- Download the matching 90-Day Action Plan at exitfactorbook.com.
- Then, put Day 1 on your calendar—before you close this book.

Chapter 10

OWN YOUR BUSINESS. OWN YOUR LIFE.

As I've told you, I wasn't raised to be an entrepreneur. I didn't come from a wealthy background; my parents are a retired nurse and an educator. We were middle-class at best. I didn't attend a fancy college, and I wasn't valedictorian. Like you, there were no handouts for me, no legs-up, and no piles of money to help.

So, how did I build a valuable business and life? First, I learned early on that building a business is just a means to an end. It's about (and yes, I'll repeat it) the time, money, and freedom it provides you.

Let me leave you with one last story, a moment that reminded me exactly why I built my business the way I did. And why this book and this program matter.

The Exit Factor

It was September 15, 2024. I had deals in motion, clients to serve, over 100 employees counting on me, and a toddler about to turn three. But that day, I had one priority:

Bruce Springsteen was coming home to Asbury Park, and there was no way I was going to miss it.

For my fellow Jersey people, like him or not, you know Bruce is the ultimate Jersey Shore bar band. He spurred hundreds, if not thousands, of bands after him that have performed in Jersey Shore bars until dawn. There is something infectious about a great bar band: the energy they create, the camaraderie among the crowd. Bruce is the master of that. And there was no way I would miss him doing it on his home turf, for what could be the last time.

My sister and I were lucky enough to be in the eighth row (out of 40,000 fans). It was a perfect night, with a full moon, and he played all of my favorite songs…including one I had been waiting to hear for over twenty years. At one point, someone even mistook me for Jessica Springsteen, a compliment I'll take.

That night is one of the top three nights of my life and will probably be until the day I die. What if I missed it?

So here's the real question:
What are you missing right now because
your business won't let you walk away?

This book isn't really about preparing you for exit. This is about giving you the freedom of choice. To choose when you work, when you rest, and what memories you create.

To attend that concert, I walked away from my business for a week and spent thousands on the trip, only to come home to a **fuller bank account and a business stronger than when I left it.**

That's the freedom I want for you: true choice, without guilt or fear. Not just the ability to walk away for a concert, but the freedom to choose how you spend your time without worrying that your business will fall apart.

Ultimately, the one thing that you, I, and every entrepreneur on this planet have in common is this: we started our businesses to have freedom of choice. To be free to spend our time how we want, serve the customers and community we want, and live our lives how we want.

Whether it's a concert, a road trip, a Michelin dinner, or simply school drop-offs, you deserve to have that freedom. I don't want money, time, or commitments to get in the way of that choice. I know that this program will provide you with those things.

These businesses are not our legacy.

Our lives, our families, and the memories we create…that's our legacy.

That night reminded me of why I built my business this way: to create memories, live freely, and never have to choose work over life. That's the freedom I want you to have too.

Because when you look back on your life, I promise, it's the memories over the meetings that will matter most. **The business is just a means to that.**

I want you to have those, and I don't want you to miss out or wake up twenty years from now regretting that you didn't take action sooner. I know you can build a business that gives you the time to enjoy life, the money to support your family, and the freedom to choose how and when you exit.

Don't stall out now. You've come this far. Don't become one of those business owners who's "five years out" for the next fifteen. If you want freedom, you can't just hope for it; you have to plan for it.

So, here's what I want you to do…right now. Think of one memory you've been putting off. A trip. A dinner. A quiet morning with your kids. A thing you say "someday" about. Schedule it. Book it. Commit to it.

This is your move now:

- Take just one small step toward the business you want.
- Revisit your scorecard.
- Assign one role.
- Block one hour.

That's how it starts: tiny shifts that create total freedom. Let this be the first thing your business makes possible, not the thing it always postpones.

We only get one life. One shot to get it right. Make sure your business provides you with the opportunity to truly live it.

BONUS 1

What to Do Next

If this book has inspired you to take action in your business or your life, I am honored. Here are some powerful options for you to fully integrate The Exit Factor program into your life and join our community, a group of exited owners, or become a certified consultant.

Option 1: Download Your Exit Factor Toolkit

If you haven't already, grab your free tools at exitfactorbook.com.

This includes:

- The Value Vision Map
- The Profit Pulse Plan
- The Role Release Roadmap
- The 3-Growth Matrix
- The Exit Prep Scorecard
- An Overview of The Exit Assessment

These are the same tools we use with all of our clients to plan, prep, and execute life-changing exits.

Option 2: Talk to Someone Who Gets It

Not sure where to begin? Or just want a sounding board? Book a free strategy call with an Exit Factor Certified Consultant at exitfactor.com/schedule-consultation.

We'll help you:

- Get clear on your exit options.
- Identify roadblocks and quick wins.
- Decide if you need a guide or just a better plan.

Option 3: Join the Exit Factor Community

Surround yourself with other business owners who are building toward freedom, just like you.

We offer exclusive content, live workshops, and early access to resources. Join at: exitfactorbook.com.

Bonus: Want to Help Business Owners Exit on Their Terms?

If this book lit a fire in you, not just for your own exit, but to help others do the same, we'd love to talk.

Exit Factor is expanding globally, and we're always seeking passionate entrepreneurs, consultants, and advisors who want to help business owners enhance their value and freedom.

Our franchisees and certified consultants are trained to help business owners increase value, reclaim time, and exit on their terms. Whether you're a coach, advisor, accountant, or former business owner, owning an Exit Factor location or becoming a certified consultant could be your next great chapter.

Learn more at: exitfactorfranchise.com

BONUS 2

Your Business Challenges, Solved

Wherever you're starting from, Exit Factor meets you there. Use this guide to identify your biggest challenge and see exactly where to focus inside the VORTEx model and Exit Factor toolkit to make real progress.

YOUR CHALLENGE	VORTEX PHASE	EXIT FACTOR TOOL OR ACTION
I'm overwhelmed and stuck working in my business every day.	Record	Role Release Roadmap
My business isn't profitable enough to sell.	Optimize	Profit Pulse Plan
I don't know what my business is worth.	Value	Exit Assessment
I'm not sure who would be interested in buying my business.	Exit	Exit Prep Scorecard
I've never thought seriously about exiting before.	Value	Value Vision Map
My team depends too much on me to operate.	Record	Role Release Roadmap
I want to exit in 2–3 years, but I'm not ready yet.	The Next 90 Days	90-Day Action Plan

YOUR CHALLENGE	VORTEX PHASE	EXIT FACTOR TOOL OR ACTION
I'm afraid that if I list my company, no one will buy it.	Exit	Exit Prep Scorecard
I received an offer, but I'm unsure if it's worthwhile.	Exit	Exit Assessment
I'm not sure if I want to sell or pass my business to family.	Value	Exit Prep Scorecard
I know I want to sell, but I don't want to wait years.	Value	Value Vision Map
I have too many "what ifs" around taxes, financing, or timing.	Exit	Exit Prep Scorecard
I need to grow my business first before selling, but I don't know how.	Transform	3-Growth Matrix
I'm thinking about growing through acquisition.	Transform	3-Growth Matrix

AUTHOR'S NOTE

If *The Exit Factor* shifted your perspective: it helped you see your business more clearly, imagine new possibilities, or feel more in control of your future, thank you. Thank you for reading, for thinking critically, and for being the kind of business owner who cares enough to plan not just for the next quarter but for the legacy you're building.

This book was born from years of seeing too many amazing entrepreneurs wait too long, sell for too little, or burn themselves out before realizing their business could have worked *for* them, not the other way around. My mission is to change that story for as many people as possible.

If this book has helped you, it may also help someone else. Here are a few small ways you can make a significant impact:

Leave a Review

Even a short review on Amazon or your favorite bookseller's site makes a huge difference. It helps more owners discover this book and embark on their exit journey with clarity and confidence.

Share the Book

Know someone who's constantly on the treadmill of their business? Who's feeling stuck, burnt out, or just wants more time or freedom? Pass this book along. One dog-eared copy could be the catalyst for their next chapter.

Stay Connected

If you're not already part of our Exit Factor community, join us. You'll find tools, updates, and a group of owners committed to building businesses that work, with or without them. Find us at exitfactorbook.com.

Thank you again for allowing me to be a small part of your journey. However your exit unfolds, I hope it brings you not just value, but freedom, clarity, and a well-earned sense of peace.

To your success,
Jessica

GLOSSARY OF TERMS

3-Growth Matrix (3GM)
Exit Factor's proprietary framework for identifying the easiest and most profitable way for growing your business. Part of the Transform phase of the VORTEx Model.

Add-backs
Adjustments made to a company's financials to show true profitability by removing non-essential or owner-specific expenses.

Asset Sale
A legal way to purchase a business in which the seller's legal entity transfers assets to a buyer's entity. This type of sale provides greater protection to a buyer.

Broker (Business Broker)
A professional who helps facilitate the sale of businesses, typically used for companies under $30 million in value.

Business Appraisal
A professional evaluation of a company's worth, typically performed by a business broker, valuation expert, or certified appraiser. Often used to set a baseline value before preparing for a sale.

Business Valuation
An estimate of how much your business is worth, based on financials, risk, and market conditions at a specific point in time.

Buy-Sell Agreement
A legal contract that outlines what happens if an owner leaves, dies, or decides to sell their portion of a business.

Cap Table (Capitalization Table)
A table that shows the ownership breakdown of a company—including shareholders, equity percentages, and stock options.

Cash Flow Statement
A financial report showing how money moves in and out of the business, including operations, investing, and financing.

Chief Financial Officer (CFO)
An executive responsible for managing the financial strategy and operations of a business.

Client Concentration
A risk factor that occurs when a large portion of revenue comes from one or two clients—reducing the business's perceived stability and value.

Confidential Information Memorandum (CIM)
A document used to present detailed financial, operational, and strategic information about a business to qualified buyers.

Due Diligence
The investigative process a buyer undertakes before finalizing a deal, reviewing all aspects of the business.

Earnings Before Interest, Taxes, Depreciation, and Amortization (EBITDA)
A measure of a company's operating performance and a key factor in determining valuation for mid-size businesses.

Earnout
A deal structure in which the seller receives compensation after the sale based on future performance benchmarks.

Exit
The point at which a business owner transitions out of their business—through sale, succession, or stepping back from daily operations.

Exit Assessment
A diagnostic review (often part of Exit Factor's program) that evaluates how prepared a business is for sale or succession—across financials, operations, leadership, and risk.

Exit Factor Consultant
A certified advisor trained in the Exit Factor methodology to help business owners prepare, plan, and execute a successful exit.

Exit Options
Flexible strategies designed to help a business owner exit successfully under various circumstances—more adaptive than an "exit plan."

Exit Prep Scorecard
Exit Factor's proprietary tool that assesses how exit-ready your business is across critical value drivers.

Exit Strategist
A consultant or advisor who helps business owners prepare for and navigate the exit process.

Inspiring Future
A personal vision statement created in the Value phase of the VORTEx model that outlines the life a business owner is working toward—not just the financial goal.

Key Performance Indicator (KPI)
Quantifiable metrics used to evaluate the success of a business or team in meeting objectives.

Letter of Intent (LOI)
A non-binding document that outlines the basic terms of a proposed deal before formal due diligence and legal contracts.

Most Probable Buyer (MPB)
The buyer type most likely to purchase your business, based on size, industry, and risk profile.

Multiple
A number applied to a company's earnings to determine its valuation (e.g., 3x EBITDA).

Non-Disclosure Agreement (NDA)
A legal agreement that protects the confidentiality of shared information during a potential sale.

Private Equity (PE)
Investment firms that acquire businesses with the goal of growing and selling them for profit—often focused on larger deals.

Profit Pulse Plan (PPP)
An Exit Factor proprietary tool used to assess financial health and identify cash flow improvements within a business. Used in the Optimize phase of the VORTEx Model.

Role Release Roadmap (3R)
Exit Factor's proprietary process for owners to strategically step back from revenue, relationship, and responsibility roles in their business. Part of the Record phase of the VORTEx Model.

Seller Financing
A portion of the purchase price financed by the seller; often used to close deals when bank loans fall short.

Seller's Discretionary Earnings (SDE)
Another metric for determining an owner's earnings in a business. This is calculated by adding one working owner's salary and defined benefits to EBITDA.

Small Business Administration (SBA)
A U.S. government agency that guarantees loans for small business acquisitions, making financing more accessible.

Value Vision Map (VVM)
Exit Factor's proprietary tool that helps owners define their desired outcomes around time, money, and freedom. This is used to execute the Value phase in the VORTEx Model.

VORTEx Model
The proprietary Exit Factor methodology for building a sellable, scalable business.

VORTEx stands for:

- **V**alue
- **O**ptimize
- **R**ecord
- **T**ransform
- **Ex**it

Working Capital
The cash needed to keep the business running day-to-day—often a point of negotiation in business sales.

ACKNOWLEDGMENTS

Writing this book and living this message has been a journey of reflection, risk, and reinvention. I could not have done it alone.

To my Exit Factor corporate team, franchisees, and consultants: You are the heartbeat behind this mission. Thank you for pouring your expertise, creativity, and heart into helping business owners build lives they love. Your belief in this work inspires me every day.

To our Exit Factor clients: You trusted us with your businesses, your legacies, and often, your most vulnerable moments. Your stories shaped every chapter of this book. Thank you for letting us walk alongside you.

To my Prospere Company Partners and Team: You were the early supporters, promoters, and testers of Exit Factor. Thank you for pushing me to think outside of our comfort zone.

To my mentors and partners, Ray Titus and Andy Cagnetta: Thank you for pushing me, challenging me, and supporting me. Your insights shaped my thinking and sharpened this message.

To my writing team, Amber Vilhauer, Amber Burdett, and Amy Valentine: Thank you for turning my thoughts into eloquent words.

To Bruce Springsteen: Thank you for inspiring me to work harder, create more, and appreciate the memories and moments we have.

To my family, Jaclyn Poole, A.J. Poole, Jaime Palmer, Judy Trilli, and Jeff Palmer: Thank you for shaping me into the person and leader I have become. And for being patient when the "just one more chapter" moments turned into working through family vacations. Your support gave me the space to create.

Finally, to my rocks, Al and Brix: Thank you for holding steady during the chaos, cheering through the wins, and helping me believe in the tornado when it was still just a funnel cloud. I love building this life with you.

www.ingramcontent.com/pod-product-compliance
Lightning Source LLC
Chambersburg PA
CBHW050954050426
42337CB00051B/837